AUDUBON'S WESTERN JOURNAL

1849-1850

John Woodhouse Audubon

AUDUBON'S WESTERN JOURNAL
1849–1850

*Being the MS. record of a trip from New York to
Texas, and an overland journey through Mexico
and Arizona to the gold-fields of California*

John Woodhouse Audubon

With biographical memoir by his daughter
MARIA R. AUDUBON

Introduction by
FRANK HEYWOOD HODDER

THE UNIVERSITY OF ARIZONA PRESS
Tucson, Arizona

The text of *Audubon's Western Journal* is a direct photographic reproduction of the first edition, published in 1906 by The Arthur H. Clark Company in Cleveland, Ohio.

Copyright, 1905, by the Arthur H. Clark Company

THE UNIVERSITY OF ARIZONA PRESS

First Printing 1984
Manufactured in the U.S.A.

Library of Congress Cataloging in Publication Data

Audubon, John Woodhouse, 1812–1862.
Audubon's Western journal, 1849–1850.

Reprint. Originally published: 1st ed. Cleveland,
Ohio : A. H. Clark, 1906. (A Rio Grande Classic)
Includes index.
1. Southwest, New — Description and travel.
2. Mexico — Description and travel. 3. Overland journeys
to the Pacific. 4. United States — Description and
travel — 1848–1865. 5. California — Gold discoveries.
6. Audubon, John Woodhouse, 1812–1862. I. Title.
II. Title: Western journal.
F786.A9 1984   917.9'042   83-17860

ISBN 0-8165-0840-2
ISBN 0-8165-0841-0 (pbk.)

CONTENTS

ILLUSTRATIONS

INTRODUCTION

ORDINARILY events are the result of antecedent causes, but now and then an apparently fortuitous incident upsets all calculations and changes the course of history in a day. Of such a character was the discovery of gold in California. It would be difficult to overstate its importance. It led directly to a similar discovery in Australia and the combined output of the two fields replenished the world's stock of precious metals, shaped monetary systems, stimulated prices and powerfully affected the economic and industrial development of the last half century. Politically for the United States the discovery was the turning point in the struggle between the sections. Texas had been annexed and the South West wrung from Mexico largely for the purpose of equalizing slave and free territory by providing the South with an outlet for Western emigration comparable in extent with that possessed by the North. The instantaneous settlement of California under circumstances unfavorable to slavery produced a free state and gave the North a majority in the Senate. The attempt to recover the lost ground brought on the Kansas struggle and precipitated the war that destroyed the only real cause of antagonism between the sections. Socially the results of the discovery were not less important.

Immediately a new state was added to the Union. Ultimately the necessity of joining the new state to the older ones opened the West to settlement, built the trans-continental railways, reclaimed the desert and peopled the continent. Fifty years ago Congress was petitioned to import "thirty camels and twenty dromedaries" and their use as a means of crossing the Western deserts was seriously discussed in books and newspapers.[1] Today there is no part of this vast territory that is not within easy reach of the railroad. Of the remarkable things accomplished in the United States perhaps the most remarkable is the rapid movement of population from seaboard to seaboard, and yet this movement has been strangely neglected by historians. They follow minutely the course of Coronado and Radisson but know little of J. S. Smith and scarcely take the trouble to trace the routes of even so famous an explorer as John C. Fremont. They devote much space to the difficulties of settling Jamestown and Plymouth and very little to the hardships of the overland journey. They carefully trace the campaigns of the War of 1812 but barely mention the wars that have won the continent from the Indians. As throwing a side-light upon one phase of this neglected movement Audubon's "Journal" is presented to the public. But quite apart from this, the book is interesting as a

---

[1] An experiment with camels was tried and proved a failure.

human document. Not only does it reflect the energy and strength of character of the author but the glimpse it gives of the constancy of the greater part of his companions and of man's humanity to man under the most trying circumstances strengthens faith in the essential soundness of human nature.

The Californian discovery was made in January of 1848. Wildly exaggerated rumors of what had been found reached the Eastern states by the middle of the following September. Official reports were received in Washington in time for mention in the President's annual message of December 5. The rush to California had already begun. As the continent could not be crossed in the winter, the earliest to start went by water. Large numbers embarked upon the long and dreary voyage around the Horn or rushed to Panama and Nicaragua to take ship from the Pacific seaports. As the spring opened, crowds collected at Independence, Missouri, ready to begin the overland journey in May, which was as early as it was safe to start. There were two overland routes from this point. The northern one followed the Oregon Trail to Fort Hall and from there crossed by way of the Humboldt River and over the Sierra Nevadas to California. The southern route followed the Santa Fé Trail to Santa Fé, where the emigrants divided, a part taking the "Old Spanish Trail" to the north and a part General Kearny's route along the Gila on the south. While some of the emigrants went as individuals, by far the larger number went in companies. Stock was subscribed to meet expenses, often by men who did not go in person, and the companies were organized for mutual assistance and defense. The company which Mr. Audubon joined was financed by his friends, the Kingslands, and was to be led by Col. Henry L. Webb. Colonel Webb, a New Yorker by birth, had joined the volunteers from Illinois at the outbreak of the Mexican war, and later had been promoted to the command of a regiment. Having served in Mexico, he knew something of the country. Partly for this reason but chiefly no doubt in order to get an earlier start, the company was to take the Mexican route. The wisdom of the choice might have been vindicated but for the loss of life and the delay caused by the cholera. This scourge was not, however, confined to the southern routes. Carried up by the river boats to Independence, it attacked the emigrants before leaving on their journey and, pursuing them to the mountains, lined the roads across the plains with newly made graves.

Leaving New York, February 8, 1849, with about eighty men and a capital of $27,000, Mr. Audubon proceeded by water to Philadelphia and Baltimore, took the railroad to Cumberland and

thence crossed the Alleghanies by stage to Brownsville and Pittsburg. Here the company took a
river boat for Cairo, where they were joined by
Colonel Webb. Changing boats they descended
the Mississippi to New Orleans, which they
reached February 18, ten days after leaving New
York. After some time spent here in the purchase
of supplies, they took a boat for Brazos at the
mouth of the Rio Grande. From Brazos they
were carried up the Rio Grande to a point opposite
Rio Grande City, where they landed on the tenth
of March. Here they were attacked by the cholera and ten men succumbed to the dread disease.
To add to their distress, the company's money was
stolen and only after great difficulty was a part
of it recovered. Discouraged by disease and mis-
fortune, twenty of the men turned back. Then
Colonel Webb deserted his company, the men at
the same time refusing to go on under his leader-
ship. For a time it seemed that the journey would
be abandoned but about half of the men asked Mr.
Audubon to lead them and bound themselves to
go on under his command. More than a month
was required for reorganization and for the recovery of the sick, so that it was not until April 28
that the start was really made. They were now
as late as the emigrants who started by the northern
routes, and were further from their goal.

Leaving the Rio Grande at Roma, the company took the main road to Chihuahua, passing through Monterey, Saltillo, Buena Vista, Parras, and Mapimi and reaching Parral June 18. Cholera still followed them and here claimed another victim. Mr. Audubon had been twice attacked but had been able to resist the disease. At Parral the company left the highway and struck across the mountains to Sonora. On the western slope towns were few and far between. Ures was reached August 22 and Altar September 9. Leaving Altar they entered a desert inhabited only by Indians living on lizards and grasshoppers. At the Pima villages on the Gila they reached the line of General Kearny's march, which had become the southern emigrant route. The march through the Gila valley to the Colorado proved the most trying part of the journey. With supplies for the men exhausted, without grass for the mules, and with little water for either, the limit of endurance was almost reached. Crossing the Colorado, the company turned northward through the desert to the mountain passes and then southward to San Diego, whence they followed the trail to Los Angeles. Here Mr. Audubon decided to send the greater part of the company to San Francisco by sea, while he, with ten of the men, drove the mules through by land. Crossing the coast range the route now followed the Tulare valley and the San Joaquin

River to Stockton. At San Francisco the company was reunited and from here started for a tour of the southern mines. Finding that they were already crowded and that the first fruits had been gathered, Mr. Audubon turned with his friend Layton to the northern mines. The two proceeded to Sacramento and thence to Coloma and Georgetown, where the journal suddenly stops. The trip was probably interrupted at this point and Mr. Audubon called back to San Francisco to make preparations for his return home.

Throughout the whole of this long journey Mr. Audubon took notes of scenes and occurrences by the way. In his descriptions he exhibits the keen observation of the naturalist and the trained eye of the artist. The result is a remarkable picture of social conditions in Mexico, of birds and trees, of sky and mountains and the changing face of nature, of the barrenness of the desert and the difficulties of the journey, of the ruined missions of California, of methods of mining, and of the chaos of races and babel of tongues in the gold fields. It was manifestly impossible to keep a daily journal, and the entries were made from time to time as opportunity occurred. Considering the circumstances under which they were taken, the notes are remarkable for their accuracy. It was Mr. Audubon's intention to rewrite and to publish them in ten parts. One part was printed privately and given to a few friends but distractions at home prevented the continuance of the work.   The notes were taken in a series of little books from which they have been faithfully transcribed by his daughter. The only omissions are a few personal references, which form no essential part of the narrative and which she has thought best not to print.   A few corrections have been made in the orthography of common words which were misspelled as a result of the haste in which they were written. Where names of places and Spanish words were spelled phonetically, the correct forms have been enclosed in brackets or given in notes at the places where they first occur.   In all essential respects the notes are printed exactly as they were left by their author.   Many of the names of places are names of haciendas and ranchos, some of which could not be identified.   Of those identified, there is some variation in spelling upon the Mexican maps of the period.   A few notes have been added chiefly in explanation of personal references in the text. The great bulk of Mr. Audubon's sketches was lost.   A few of those that were saved have been reproduced and a portrait of Mr. Audubon, taken in 1853, has been added, together with a map of his route.   F. H. H.

BIOGRAPHICAL MEMOIR

BIOGRAPHICAL MEMOIR

JOHN WOODHOUSE AUDUBON, the younger of the two sons of John James Audubon and his wife, Lucy Bakewell, was born in Henderson, Kentucky, November 30, 1812. Those who recall the life of the ornithologist may remember that at this time he was far from his days of prosperity, and was trying to be a business man, with saw-mills and lumber; a venture, which like all his business efforts, did not succeed. Therefore, almost before the boy John remembered, the wandering days began for him, which continued virtually all his life. During his boyhood these wanderings were chiefly confined to that portion of the United States south of the Ohio River, and largely to Louisiana, a section of country he always loved.

As a child, though small and slender, he was strong and active and delighted in the open air life which was indeed his second nature; and he was proficient in swimming, shooting, fishing and all out-door sports and pleasures, while still a boy. He was rather averse to the needful studies which kept him from the woods and streams, but which his mother never permitted him to neglect. She was, herself, the teacher of her sons in their earlier years, and a most thorough one, as later generations can testify, sending them to school only when she realized that they needed contact with boys of their own age; but the home education was never given up.   Both she and Mr. Audubon were excellent musicians, great readers, and most desirous that their children should be prepared, as fully as possible, to enter the world as educated, and even accomplished men.   Drawing was an important matter always, and both sons, Victor and John, became well skilled in this art, but in different lines, the first in landscape, the second in delineating birds and quadrupeds — or as the scientists say today, mammals — the latter being his specialty, though the first intention was that he should be a portrait painter.

The boys while children were usually together, and were sent to school at the same time, though Victor was three years the elder, but at times they were separated.   Victor was a quiet, studious boy, and a great favorite with the elder members of his mother's family, the Bakewells, while John, who was full of mischief, very restless, always most successful in getting his young cousins as well as himself into all sorts of scrapes, was naturally less in demand.   When Mr. and Mrs. Audubon were wandering from place to place, Victor was frequently with relatives in Louisville, and at an early age became a clerk in the office of Mr. Nicholas Berthoud, who had married a sister of Mrs. Audubon.   He was in this position when

his father sailed for England in 1826, while John
remained in Louisiana with his mother at Bayou
Sara, where she was then teaching.

At this period of his life John spent much time
drawing from nature, and playing the violin, of
which he was passionately fond all his life. While
his father was pushing the publication of "The
Birds of America" in England and Scotland, he
at one time supplemented the slender finances of
the family, in a small way, by taking occasional
trips on the Mississippi river steamboats as a clerk.
It was very uncongenial work to the restless youth,
and, from what can be learned, was rather indifferently done; but he was a great favorite with all
with whom he came in contact, and usually found
some one to help him over his mistakes, and indeed
on occasion to do his work, while he, with his violin
was in great demand on the decks of the steamboats, in those days scenes of much gaiety, some of
which was of more than doubtful quality. After a
comparatively short season of mingled work and
play, Mrs. Audubon withdrew him from what
Louisianians called "the river," and he returned to
his work in painting and in collecting specimens
which his father wanted for the various friends and
scientists with whom he was now constantly in
touch.

The elder Audubon upon his return from
Europe took the family, after a few weeks in

Louisiana, further north, and they were some time in the vicinity of Philadelphia and New York. In 1830 the two brothers were left in America while Mr. and Mrs. Audubon were in England and France, and again John tried his hand at clerkship with better success than in his earlier years, but not for long.

On his return to America Mr. Audubon made plans for a summer in Labrador and in 1833 made this journey, John with three other young men accompanying him. The days were not only long, but arduous. John was not quite twenty-one, and his love of fun was as strong as in his boyhood, but he found none in being called at three in the morning to search for birds, being frequently drenched to the skin all day, and working with bird skins through "the interminable twilights." Nevertheless he and his young companions found time to rob salmon preserves when the fishermen would not sell, to slip on land when opportunity offered, to attend some of the very primitive balls and other amusements to be found on these desolate shores, and to extract pleasures which perhaps youth alone could have found among such surroundings.

So passed the years taking boyhood and youth with them until 1834, when the Audubon family all went to England and Scotland, where both young men painted very steadily, making copies of many of the celebrated pictures within reach of which they now found themselves. At this time John confined himself almost wholly to copying portraits, principally those of Sir Thomas Lawrence, whose friendship was most valuable to him, of Van Dyke and Murillo, and, when in Edinburgh, giving great attention to the beautiful work of Sir Henry Raeburn. Some of these early pictures are still in the possession of the family, though many were sold and many given away. He also painted some water colors of birds, which are said to be good work by those who know them.

This period of study was broken, however, by a trip to the continent taken by the brothers together. The route followed was the one then called "The Grand Tour," extending as far as Italy. The brothers, always most closely united, congenial in thoughts and tastes, thoroughly enjoyed the novel scenes and experiences, for which they were well fitted both physically and mentally. They were tall, handsome young men, full of health and strength, and the joyousness of youth. The careful preparation in the reading of books of travel and literature, and the fact that they were excellent French scholars, added greatly to the interest of the journey.

But busier days than these were in store, when the Audubons returned to America, and the collection of new species demanded the attention of the naturalist, and the assistance of his sons. Victor attended to most of the business details, partly in England and partly in America, while my father and grandfather searched the woods, and in 1836 went as far south as the Gulf of Mexico. It was at the beginning of this trip that, passing through Charleston, a visit was paid to the home of Dr. John Bachman, and the attachment began between my father and Maria Bachman, which resulted in their marriage in 1837.

Shortly after John and his young wife went to England, where his father had again gone to superintend the continued publication of the plates in London, and here their first child, Lucy, was born. Six months later, John with his wife and child returned to America. The next two years were spent partly in New York, partly in the south, in the vain hope of finding health and strength for the delicate young mother, but all was unavailing, and she died leaving two little daughters, one an infant. Later John Audubon married an English lady, Caroline Hall, and to them seven children were born, five of whom lived to maturity.

At this time the country place on the Hudson river near New York City, which had been bought in 1840, was built upon. Today it is well nigh lost in the rapidly advancing streets and avenues, but at this time it was almost primitive forest, and here for some years lived the naturalist and his wife, with the two sons and their respective families. It is hard today to picture the surroundings of that time. No railroad cut off the waters of the lovely river, than the highway from the avenue to Albany, and alive with craft of many kinds. The other three sides were heavily wooded; and neighbors there were none, for it was not until some years later that other homes began slowly to appear here and there. Few if any of the friends of the Audubons in those days are left on earth, and the houses where they once lived have, with few exceptions, either been torn down or so altered that their former owners would not recognize them.

Minniesland with its large gardens and orchards, especially celebrated for peaches, its poultry yards and dairy which added to the comfort of the home and of the many guests who always found a welcome there, had an interesting side in the elk, deer, moose, foxes, wolves and other wildwood creatures which were kept for study and pleasure; and still another in the books, pictures and curios within the ever hospitable house, but more than all was the charm of the tall gray-haired old man, who by talent, industry, and almost incredible perseverance won it for those he loved.

The early days at Minniesland were very happy ones for all. The "Quadrupeds of North America" had been begun and was of intense interest to father and sons, and the work he was doing for this publication, the superintendence of the animal life about the home, the varied enjoyments and duties of the country place gave my father ample occupation. He loved the Hudson and the Palisades, the woods and walks about him, was devoted to his family and these were years he delighted to recall.

Many men were employed in one capacity or another and "Mr. John," as he was always called, was a great favorite. He had the rare gift of keeping these men friends, while he was perfectly understood to be the master; they were thoroughly at home with him, yet never familiar, and this position, so difficult to maintain, he held with all. As the village of Manhattanville, a little lower down the river, grew in size, many of the men from there used to walk up on summer evenings to help "haul the seine;" for fish were plentiful and good in the Hudson then; and where "Mr. John" was, disturbance or insolence was unknown, his orders to each man were respected, his division of fish always satisfied.

An interruption in this tranquil life came in 1843 when Audubon the elder went to the Yellowstone country, and both sons were anxious about their father until his return; they felt that he was too old for such an arduous journey, but he was determined to go, and his safe return ended all alarm for his safety. Another break came in 1845 when my father went to Texas to find mammals to depict in the new work being published, and possibly birds

not yet described. He took with him as sole
companion of his travels James B. Clement, one
of the men about the place, in whom he had — and
most justly — perfect confidence. He was in
Texas many months, travelling quite extensively,
and at a time when the Indians were not friendly.
Even more danger might be apprehended from the
white men of desperate character, who had drifted
to that region either to escape punishment for
previous crimes, or to find themselves so far from
law and order that they could commit fresh ones
in safety. It was on this trip that my father met
Colonel Hays, well known then as "Jack Hays the
Texan Ranger," between whom and himself a
strong friendship was formed, and to whom my
father felt much indebted; as, knowing the country
so well, Colonel Hays gave him valuable aid in
choosing routes, selecting Indians as guides and
hunters, and in avoiding camps and settlements
where he would certainly have been robbed, and
possibly murdered, had he offered to protect his
possessions, for at that time all money had to be
carried in coin.

Upon this journey my father was very successful
in securing specimens. When he returned he
brought one of his hunters, a half-breed Indian
named Henry Clay, a name which had probably
been given to him in jest. This man was my
father's shadow; he was very skillful in the care of

the animals, a splendid boatman and fisherman and very valuable about the place. But civilization was too wearisome for him, he left two or three times and came back, but about 1852 returned to Texas with Captain McCown.[1]

In 1846, the year following the Texan journey, John Audubon with his wife and children went to Europe, in order that he might paint pictures — still for the "Quadrupeds" — from some of the specimens he could find only in the zoological collections of London, Paris and Berlin, and he was absent on this work more than a year and a half. It was a period of most arduous work; his letters home were very short, though he was an easy and rapid writer. The reason for this brevity was, as he often explains, that his arm and hand were tired with the long days of steady painting; particularly when the fur of the animals he was delineating was of unusual length, for this was before the days of "dabs and smudges" and minuteness of detail was insisted on both by the elder Audubon and by the engravers. These were long months to him as most of them were passed in crowded cities, where he missed the forests and rivers, his home and the free life to which he was accustomed. Many times in the letters written to those at Minniesland, he declares his intention

---

[1] John Porter McCown resigned his commission in 1861 to join the Confederate army, in which he served through the war as a major general. — F. H. H.

of never leaving home again, an intention he was
unable to carry out.

In 1849 he joined a California company, being
urged thereto by the Messrs. Kingsland, who were
warm personal friends and who were then backing
Col. Henry L. Webb who had been in Mexico and
advocated that route for the company he was
collecting. My father's idea was that such a journey offered splendid opportunities to secure specimens of birds and mammals. It was proposed
that he should give the company his knowledge of
a backwoodsman's life, which was extensive, and
be second in command to Colonel Webb, a respon
sibility which he rather hesitated to accept, as he
wished the freedom of leaving the party anywhere
he chose after reaching California. Finally,
however, he signed papers with Messrs. Daniel C.
and Ambrose Kingsland, and Cornelius Sutton,
(Colonel Webb signing also), to stay with the
company for one year, when they expected to reach
their destination and be on the high road to wealth.

In Colonel Webb's company the contracts were
individual. The company supplied everything
but the personal belongings of each man and his
horse, and he in return was supposed to repay with
legal interest his share of expenses when he reached
the El Dorado, and to this end his work and his
earnings were the company's for a year from the
time of signing. If when the contracts expired

there were any profits, these were to be divided in a certain ratio. My father's contract was signed January 31, 1849, and the fact that he was going induced many of his personal friends and acquaintances to join also. Almost all the men employed at Minniesland went with "Mr. John." To the daughter of one of these, Mrs. Alice Walsh Tone, I am much indebted for help in names and dates.

The journey across the continent in 1849 with no regular means of communication with home and friends, through a country virtually unknown, and when Indians were still numerous; without cities to enable travelers to get fresh supplies of food and clothing, and with no very definite knowledge of the road, was a serious matter under the best of conditions and on the best route. What it was with men who, with few exceptions, knew nothing of the life before them, who were impoverished by robbery, discouraged by death and disease and deserted by their leader, upon a route of which my father never approved, may be best learned from his "Journal." The journey was a terrible disappointment to him, as he says: "my arsenic is broadcast on the barren clay soil of Mexico, the paper in which to preserve plants was used for gun-wadding, and, though I clung to them to the last, my paints and canvases were left on the Gila desert of awful memories."

In July, 1850, he sailed for home, which he

reached in safety after the delay of a week at the Isthmus of Panama. Most unfortunately all his paintings, which were of course sketches to be worked up from notes, and most of the water colors he had made, nearly two hundred in all, had to be left temporarily at Sacramento; later they were taken to San Francisco and Mr. Robert Simson took charge of them for a time. He entrusted them, at my father's request, to Mr. John Stevens and with that noble man and true friend they went down in the wreck of the steamer "Central America."

It would be interesting to follow the careers of those who made the California journey with my father, but the lapse of fifty-six years makes this almost impossible, and very few traces of the members of the party can be found, nor indeed can any full list of those who left New Orleans with him be made. James B. Clement remained in Stockton as did Nicholas Walsh and John H. Tone; they became fruit growers and were successful in the land of their adoption. Henry C. Mallory entered business in San Francisco, married and lived in that city until his death, now a number of years ago. Robert Simson died not long since; he lived for some time in San Francisco, being a partner in a legal firm, afterwards removing to Alameda. He married rather late in life, and left a widow and one son. Langdon Havens returned to his home at Fort Washington and many others also came back to the east. The greater part of the company, I believe, remained upon the Pacific Slope; but I have been unable to locate them or their descendants, except in the few instances I have mentioned. Though the company proved an utter failure financially, yet nearly every man eventually reimbursed the Messrs. Kingsland for their outlay, and in five instances the friends of those who died did for them that, which living they would doubtless have done for themselves.

At the time of the California journey my father was thirty-six, tall, strong and alert though always slender, keen of vision and hearing, quick in movement and temperament, and with most tender and skillful hands as those have testified whom he nursed in the dreadful cholera days. He had inherited from his father the gift of making and keeping friends among all classes, and of giving them confidence in him — the result of his quick and deep sympathy, his unselfishness and his absolute truthfulness. He was never indolent; whatever work had to be done, his was the hardest part — he never shirked, never grumbled. As evidence of this trait of his character I quote from one of his companions, Lieutenant Browning, whose son has kindly given me some extracts from his letters: "Mr. Audubon is always doing somebody's else work as well as his own;" "Mr. Audubon never thinks of himself, I never knew such a big-hearted man." I will touch on only one other characteristic. He was subject to periods of the deepest depressions, a trait also inherited from his father, which sometimes weighed his spirits down for days, and which it seemed impossible for him to dispel. Often on this California journey the effort to appear bright and cheerful when he was in one of these moods physically exhausted him, and in some of his letters he speaks of the relief it was when night came and he was alone, and had no need to look or be other than he felt. He never outlived these attacks as the naturalist did, perhaps because his life was so much shorter.

My father's home-coming showed him many sad changes, for his father was now not only an old but a broken man, and the spirit of the home was no longer joyous. Father, mother, and sons had always been most united, unusually so it seems, as many incidents and events are recalled. Possibly this deep affection was the result of the struggles of early days, which, throwing them so much on each other for companionship, developed a sympathy with one another which lives full of separate interests would not have fostered — possibly the great similarity of work and tastes drew them closer to each other than when such conditions do not exist, but whatever the reason, it is certain that the ties which held them together were never loosened but by death; and so, when in January, 1851, he who had been the light of the home passed away, the break was most keenly and deeply felt.

In 1853 two new houses near the original one, now grown too small for the many children, were completed and these Victor and John Audubon occupied with their families, the mother living with one son or the other as the spirit moved her. The continued publication of "The Quadrupeds" and the octavo edition of "The Birds" occupied both my uncle and father. The latter reduced all the large plates of the birds to the desired size by means of the *camera lucida,* his delicate and exact work fitting him for the exquisitely minute details required. Much of each winter was spent in the southern states, securing subscribers.

In 1853 a great sorrow came in the death of a little daughter, and soon after even a heavier. Victor Audubon began to fail in health, the result of a fall which at the time was thought to be of no moment, but which had injured the spine. Through long years it was agony to my father to witness the constant decline of the brother with whom his entire life was so intimately associated and to whom he was so deeply attached. Nothing could stay the progress of the malady and on the seventeenth of August, 1860, came the parting which had so long been dreaded.

During this long period of my uncle's illness all

the care of both families devolved on my father. Never a "business man," saddened by his brother's condition, and utterly unable to manage at the same time a fairly large estate, the publication of two illustrated works, every plate of which he felt he must personally examine, the securing of subscribers and the financial condition of everything— what wonder that he rapidly aged, what wonder that the burden was overwhelming! After my uncle's death matters became still more difficult to handle, owing to the unsettled condition of the southern states where most of the subscribers to Audubon's books resided, and when the open rupture came between north and south, the condition of affairs can hardly be imagined, except by those who lived through similar bitter and painful experiences.

Worn out in body and spirit, overburdened with anxieties, saddened by the condition of his country, it is no matter of surprise that my father could not throw off a heavy cold which attacked him early in 1862. On the evening of Tuesday, February 18, he was playing on his violin some of the Scotch airs of which he was so fond, when suddenly putting down the instrument he said he had so much fever he would retire. Before morning delirium set in, and for two days and nights he wandered in spirit over the many lands where once in health and strength the happy boy, the joyous youth, the earnest man had traveled in body. Especially was the Californian trip present in his fevered mind, and incidents and scenes were once more vividly before him, until on the twenty-first he fell asleep never to awaken here, and, as the stormy night closed in, almost at the same hour as that on which his father died, he too took the last journey and entered into that unknown land, and was "forever free from storm and stress." His forty-nine years of life had been very full ones, he had touched the extremes of joy and sorrow, he had known failure and success; like his father he had never done anything indifferently. His enthusiasm carried him over many difficulties, his sympathy and generosity endeared him to every one and, when the end of the busy life came, there was left a vacant place, never to be filled, in the hearts of those who knew and loved him.

MARIA R. AUDUBON

SALEM, NEW YORK, March 2, 1905.

AUDUBON'S WESTERN JOURNAL

1849-1850

CHAPTER I

A YEAR of quiet at my happy home had passed since my return from my last voyage to England, when "the fever" as it was called began to rage in New York, and as I sat, convalescent from a fever of a different kind at the time, of more danger than my present trip, I listened to the tales of speedily accumulated fortunes. At first I heard them with complete scepticism, again with less, until in some degree faith in the tales began to be awakened in my mind, and at last I thought it might possibly come to pass that I should go to California; but still it was very vague, and I scarcely dwelt on the idea of so long a trip except as a dream. However, I mentioned it to two or three of my friends asking what they thought, and answers came, as is always the case on occasions when advice is asked, so various, that I was bewildered, and finally I felt I must come to those in my own home to aid me in my decision. But even here I was thrown back upon my own judgment. My noble father could give me no advice now, but in 1845, when I was in Texas, he had written to me: "Push on to California, you will find new animals and birds at every change in the formation of the country, and birds from Central America will delight you."

After long talks over the "pros and cons," I concluded to go for a long eighteen months from my beloved home, and decided to join "Col. H. L. Webb's California Company" which was being organized. I was appointed second in command owing to my knowledge of backwoodsman's life and the experience of my Texas trip; and after eight weeks of weariness and anxiety found I was to take charge of eighty men and, with $27,000.00 belonging to the Company, was to meet Col. Webb at Cairo.

I had talked with fathers, and with young men who wished to learn all about a backwoodsman's life in half an hour, made purchases of arms and implements and various needful articles, and finally all was ready, and the date of departure decided upon.

Feb. 8th, 1849. A day of hurry began, and three o'clock found us on board the steamer "Transport," surrounded by the company and a crowd of their friends and ours to see us off. Fathers took my hands in both theirs, and in scarcely audible voices begged me to take care of only sons, brothers asked me to give counsel and advice to younger brothers, men I had never seen gave hearty hand clasps that told of sound hearts, and said: "My brother's with you, treat him right and if he is *my* brother he'll die for you, or with you." The final words of clergymen as they gave us their parting advice and blessing, were drowned by the tolling of the last bell. Its knell went to my heart like a funeral note, and I was too much overcome to answer the cheer of the hundreds who came down to see us off, and in silence waved my cap to my brother and friends, and in deep mental sorrow prayed God for courage and ability to do all I had promised to try to do.

My men looked back to New York's beautiful battery, and I paced the boiler deck almost alone, watching the red sunset and cooling my burning face and aching head with the north-west wind, cold and frosty from the snow covered palisades, turning often to look up "our North River" to see if I could get one glimpse of that home so long to be unseen.

The tide was low so we had to take the outside, and I went to the bow to look over Sandy Hook towards the broad Atlantic, and to try to realize that the Pacific had to be seen before I could again return to my own beautiful coast. It was a most curious sight as I entered the cabin of the boat to see the different feelings exhibited; some were in deep thought; some in sorrowful anxiety; some gay, and again others with evidently forced merriment; but in the main, cheerfulness was certainly on every side, and when I had to announce that we had been promised what was not on board, a good supper, not a murmur was heard, and merriment was created by the imitations of the orders of the New York eating-houses such as: "roast beef rare," "plum pudding both kinds of sauce," etc.

Our cabins were not the most comfortable, nor was the floor of the dining saloon too soft for some of our city men, but we slept soundly from one until four; took breakfast at five, and at eight were driving in the quiet, dignified streets of Philadelphia towards the Schuylkill. Very cold weather had followed us, and the heavy northwester of the day previous retarded our progress across the Chesapeake from Frenchtown.[1] At Baltimore we took our luggage at once to the railroad station, and went to the United States and Union Hotels, where for a dollar and a quarter each we had supper, bed and breakfast, and went off, all in better spirits, for Cumberland, where, after a miserable dinner and supper combined, we packed into fourteen stages, having paid nearly an average of two dollars each for extra luggage, fifty pounds being the regular allowance for each man.

Feb. 10th. Fortunately we had a full moon, and as the mountains were all ice and snow it was

---

[1] Frenchtown was the western terminus of the New Castle and Frenchtown Railroad, one of the first railroads built in the United States and a part of the early route between the East and the West. With the passing of the road, the town entirely disappeared. It was located at the head of the Elk River branch of Chesapeake Bay, below the present site of Elkton.

"as light as day." Overloaded, and with top-heavy coaches, on our hind wheels would keep slipping first on one side, then on the other, to see what the front ones were doing, it was most extraordinary we did not capsize, all of us; but no accident occurred, and at eight next morning we had descended Laurel Hill on a run, and were slowly winding the lanes of a more civilized country.

As it was Sunday, many cheerful groups, gaily dressed, ornamented the stoops and sunny sides of the houses and barns of the contented farmers of western Pennsylvania, as we passed on to Browns-ville, where we arrived at noon, glad enough to be safely landed on the banks of the Monongahela. We reached Pittsburgh at nine the same evening, went to the Monongahela House and had a comfortable supper, but as most of our luggage was on the steamer for Cincinnati, I went on board and took my berth.

Morning came, and after a few kind words from my relations at Pittsburgh, we left, and had one of the hundreds of monotonous voyages down the Ohio that are yearly performed by the steamers. At Cincinnati I was met by two additional volunteers, engaged by Col. Webb, and was much pleased by their appearance, though I should have preferred seeing backwoodsmen and men who knew more of the life we were going to lead, but we must hope on, and trust to Providence.

Passages and fares at hotels, etc., included, were now calculated to see how we had estimated the cost of each person to Cairo, and we found that for each one it was one dollar and forty-five cents over the twenty-five dollars allowed, and I took passages to the latter place direct, remaining only four hours at Louisville, where I had the good fortune to find my uncle W. G. Bakewell waiting for me, and dined with him while our boat was putting out some freight at Albany, below the falls. When I joined my party I was told that some of the men had stolen a valuable pointer dog, and that a telegraphic notice had been sent after them; but on inquiring I found it had been purchased, no doubt from a thief, so we sent it back from Cairo.

Large flocks of geese and ducks were seen by us as we made the mouth of the Ohio, and the numbers increased about Cairo. The ice in the Mississippi was running so thick that the "J. Q. Adams" returned after a fruitless effort to ascend the river. All Cairo was under water, the wharf boat we were put on, an old steamer, could only accommodate thirty-five of our party, so that the other thirty had to be sent to another boat of the same class; the weather was extremely cold, with squalls of snow from the north with a keen wind, there was no plank from our boat to the levee of Cairo, the only part of the city out of water. Will it be wondered at that a slight depression of spirits should for an instant assail me? But when a man has said he will do a thing it must be done if life permits, and in an hour we found ourselves by a red hot stove, the men provided with good berths for the place, cheerfulness restored, and after an hour's chat, while listening to the ever increasing gale outside, we parted for the night to wake cold, but with good appetites even for the horrible fare we had, and as young Kearney Rodgers said, as we looked at the continents of coffee-stains, and islands of grease here and there, with lumps of tallow and peaks of frozen butter on our once white table cloth, "Is it not wonderful what hunger will bring us to?"

Here we found Col. Webb with his wife and son; I was much pleased with the dignified and ladylike appearance of Mrs. Webb; once she had been very beautiful, now she was greatly worn, and had a melancholy expression, under the circumstances more appropriate than any other, for her husband and only son were about to leave her for certainly eighteen months, and perhaps she was parting with them for the last time. We chatted together in rather a forced conversation, until the "General Scott" for New Orleans came by, and then went on board paying eight dollars for each man and five dollars each for Col. Webb's three horses; so much for Cairo, I don't care ever to see it again.

I found my uncle, W. G. Bakewell, on board making the trip to New Orleans, and my journey was as agreeable as it could be, where all my associations were of a melancholy nature. I thought of past joys and friends dead and scattered since the days when I knew this country so well.

The river was very high, and the desolation of the swamps, the lonely decaying appearance of the clay bluffs, picturesque as they are, added to the eternal passing on of this mighty stream towards its doom, to be swallowed in earth's great emblem of eternity, the ocean, told only of the passing of all things.

February 18th. Four days from Cairo found us at New Orleans, and a few hours enabled me to find hotels for our party, and at six o'clock I was able to tell Col. Webb that I had done all I could that night and would be with him at nine next morning, and left for the quiet of my aunt's[1] home.

February 19th was spent in running all over New Orleans, ordering horse and mule shoes, bacon, flour, bags, tools, ammunition, and making arrangements to change our certificates of deposit for such funds as would pass in Mexico. I called with Col. Webb on General and Mrs. Gaines and was most kindly received by both, and afterwards asked to call again, but had no time, as every minute was occupied with my business.

---

[1] Mrs. Alexander Gordon.— M. R. A.

Two of our men had to be returned from this place of bars, billiards and thirsty souls, and one of our other junior boat men was dismissed because he met some of his old "friends" (?) who would insist not only on a jovial dinner, but masked balls and all the other concomitants, and after four days of this, a unanimous vote of the company expelled him.

Sunday is selected at New Orleans for the departure of vessels to all parts of the world and at ten o'clock on the morning of March the 4th, we left in the steamer "Globe" for Brazos, north of Rio Grande. We descended the river to the mouth, but anchored there, as there is a dangerous bar, and the weather not looking favorable the Captain of our frail vessel deemed it prudent to wait until dawn before attempting to go further. We left our anchorage at daybreak, the cross seas of the outer bar breaking over the bows at almost every wave, and I felt that if a real gale came up from the south-east our trip to California would soon end. The day continued as it had begun. I went to my berth and could not have been persuaded that it was not blowing hard if I had not been able to see the water from my porthole. The night came on with a full moon and the trade wind of the Gulf just fanned a ripple on the old swell to send millions of sparkling lights in petty imitation of those spangling the heavens.

Three such nights and four days of hot sun, and we were running over the bar at Brazos in only seven or eight feet of water. Not a landmark more than ten feet high was in sight, but we could see miles and miles of breakers combing and dashing on the glaring beach, broken here and there by dark, weather-stained wrecks of unfortunate vessels that had found their doom on this desolate shore.

Brazos, like Houston in 1837, is nothing if you take away what belongs to government, a long flat a mile wide, extending for a good distance towards the Rio Grande, is kept out of reach of the sea by a range of low sand hills, if drifts of eight to ten or fifteen feet deserve the name; so like those on all our low shores from Long Island to Florida that every traveller knows what the island of Brazos is. The inner bay, however, looking towards Point Isabel is beautiful, and but for the extreme heat would have given me a splendid opportunity for one of my greatest pleasures, sailing.

We found a few cases of cholera had occurred here, and Major Chapman[1] with the kindness so generally shown by our officers to their countrymen, sent off our party at once in the government steamer "Mentoria." At New Orleans I could

---

[1] William Warren Chapman was brevetted major for gallant conduct in the battle of Buena Vista, and died in 1859.

not insure our money over the bar of the Rio
Grande without an immense premium, so I, with
Biddle Boggs and James Clement, having landed
the horses brought with us, went overland from
Brazos to Brownsville opposite Matamoras, thirty-
two miles, long ones. We took all our money
with us, and started in buoyant spirits. At 10:30,
March 8th, I found myself riding along the beach
of this barren island; for six or eight miles we went
merrily on, watching the little sand-pipers and
turn-stones, and enjoying the invigorating sea-
breeze, as the sun was intensely hot, and when,
from time to time we passed through narrow lanes
of chaparral where the breeze was shut out, and
the dust followed our horses, we were exceedingly
oppressed.

We had all seen Texas before, and like sailors
once familiarized with the sea whom an hour re-
stores to old habits and thoughts, so with the man of
the prairies, and we all felt at home at once. The
country is flat, showing here and there in the distance some of those bold prominences of clay represented so beautifully by the Prince de Neuwied in
his wonderful illustrations of the West.[1] These
near the Rio Grande, are, of course, only minia-
tures of the "Chateaux blancs" of the northern

---

[1] *Travels in the Interior of North America,* by Maximilian, Prince
of Wied-Neuwied (London, 1843). Reprinted in Thwaites's
Early Western Travels, 1748-1846 (Cleveland, 1905).

Mississippi. After our long ride of thirty-two miles, with only a hard boiled egg each for our mid-day meal, at three o'clock we reached Brownsville where the rolling of bowling-alleys and the cannoning of billiard balls was all that seemed to enliven the village at that hour. I went to find the Quartermaster to know where to put our money for safety, and was most kindly received by Major Brice[1] who took charge of it and put it in the strong box at Fort Brown. From this place we had next morning a fine view of Matamoras, and the American-like appearance rather startled me from my old belief of the low standard of all things Mexican, for it was the only town like a town I had seen; but I resumed my old opinion when I was told that all the good houses had been built by Mr. McGown, who had resided there for years, and so far I have not seen anything in the shape of architecture worthy the name, except the old missions about San Antonio de Bexar.

Brownsville, March 8th. Almost a calm this clear morning, but occasionally a soft breeze, so gentle as just to wave the white cover of the table at which I sat. From time to time a distant hammer sluggishly drove a nail, and the proud cock was heard to boast his self-importance in a shrill

---

[1] Major Benjamin William Brice served through the Civil War in the paymaster's department and became a major general at its close.

crow, the same I have heard from Berlin to this lonely place; the mocking-birds sang just as they did in my happiest days in beautiful Louisiana; my heart went back to my home, and a foreboding of evil seemed to come over me.

Brownsville is one of those little places like thousands of others in our Southern states; little work and large profits give an undue share of leisure without education or refinement, consequently drinking-houses and billiards with the etc. are abundant. The river here is narrow and rapid, and crossed by two ferry-boats swung on hawsers in the old-fashioned way stretching from bank to bank of the great "Rio Grande del Norte." They do a thriving business, as Matamoras contains many Mexicans who do both a wholesale and retail "running business," that is, smuggling.

March 10th. Col. Webb and the company came up last evening on the "Mentoria," Captain Duffield. He stayed over night and after purchasing a few barrels of rice at about twice its cost at New Orleans, and one or two little additions to our already large stock of necessaries, we set sail in the "Corvette," Captain O'Daniel. Some time was lost in our progress that night, as we stuck on the bar just above the town, however we soon went on, and I found this river quite different from the usual run of its channel, as after every rise, which is not often at this season, the channel is left full of mud, and the deepest water for a week or so *outside* the regular channel.

I do not believe any part of this country can be good for a thing, as the rain is so uncertain in its favors. The miserable Mexicans, who live far apart, at distances of ten or even twenty miles from each other, do not plant their patches of corn with any certainty that it will mature, the rain failing to come to fill the ears more frequently than it comes.

The ranchos are forlorn "Jacals" (a sort of open-work shed covered with skins and rushes and plastered with mud, here so full of lime and marl that it makes a hard and lasting mortar), precisely alike, varying only in picturesqueness of tree or shrub, or rather shrub alone, for there are no fine trees here, though the musquit[1] and willow sometimes arrive at the height of twenty or twenty-five feet, and back from the river the hackberry attains a tolerable size.

A tall reed of rank growth in thickets, and in other places a dwarf willow in patches like the young cottonwoods along the banks of the Mississippi, are the chief growth.

The water is warm, and so full of lime as to create, rather than allay thirst; what but necessity

---

[1] The mesquit or mesquite is a tree, resembling the locust, of which there are several species in Mexico and the southwestern part of the United States.

could ever have induced settlers to remain here I
can not tell, for the whole trip from Brownsville
to Camp Ringgold[1] does not present one even
tolerable view; and the most pleasing sight to us
was our own bright flag, one minute fluttering in
a southeast breeze, then gently falling to its rough
flag-staff, and again, five minutes after, blowing
furiously from the northwest, so changeable are
the winds; we hoisted our flag in return, and came
to, just under Major Lamotte's[2] tent.

Col. Webb went in to see him alone, to induce
him to allow us to go as far as Roma, but it
appeared that Major Chapman had given orders
to the contrary, as our boat was so large that her
return would be doubtful, so we were taken only
two miles further up the river, and put out on the
Mexican side, on a sandbar, opposite Rio Grande
City. It was two o'clock, the sun pouring down
on us, the mercury 98 degrees in the shade, nevertheless with all our winter blood in us, we had to
unload our heavy luggage. Casks of government
tents and camp equipage, which we were obliged
to roll sixty or seventy yards through mud and
sand, was hard work. This began to tell the tale.

---

[1] Camp Ringgold was an American military post below Rio
Grande City. Davis's rancho, mentioned later, was half a
mile above Camp Ringgold.

[2] Joseph Hatch La Motte, brevetted a major for gallant
conduct at Monterey, resigned from the service in 1846 and
died in 1888.

The good men went at it with a will, the dandies looked at their hands, touched a bacon barrel, rubbed their palms together, looked again, and put on gloves; but it would not do, and out of our ninety-eight men, only about eighty were at their work with good will and cheerful hearts, but all was soon done, and I gave a sort of melancholy glance at the "Corvette" as she started off. The Captain had been very kind to us and we gave him three cheers, and turned to set up our tents for the first time. We adhered closely to military style, and our straight line of tents did not vary; dry sand or wet mud had no effect on our position. In the cool of the evening after I had done all I could for the comfort of those around me, I stretched myself out, with hat, coat and boots off, to look at the busy scene around me. Gaily and cheerfully everything went on, under a clear sky like that of August at home, with all the soft, balmy, summer-like feeling. About me were the familiar notes of dozens of mocking-birds and thrushes. I opened out the nucleus of my collections, a little package of birdskins; a new thrush, a beautiful green jay, a new cardinal, were side by side with two new wood-peckers and a little dove, all new to our fauna, and I carefully spread them out to dry, and admired them. The sun went down, our supper was ready, and never did a company enjoy their meals more than we did for the first two days we

were ashore, when exercise and good health gave
a relish to everything. Our guard was set and
detailed for the night, and I turned in on my
blankets with a short prayer for health and continuance of blessings on my family.

CHAPTER II

DISASTER IN THE VALLEY OF THE RIO GRANDE

March 13th, 1849. Daylight came in beautiful and calm, but we were enveloped in a dense fog, so heavy that though the clear sky could be seen over head, not more than fifty yards could be distinguished about us, and the tents looked as if we had had a heavy rain in the night.

Col. Webb went over to Camargo to report himself and the company to the Alcalde and returned at night with a Mr. Nimons, and it was arranged that they should go next day to China[1] to purchase mules. Rob Benson was sergeant of the guard that night, and I took a few turns around our camp with him and turned in, but about eleven was called to see J. Booth Lambert, who was very sick. Dr. Trask began to fear his illness might be cholera, but it was not in every respect like what he had seen of that disease in the north. At three o'clock, however, he seemed much easier and more composed, alas, the composure of cholera. What does it foretell? But in this instance to me "ignorance was bliss." At five I was up again, mustard plasters, rubbing and a tablespoonful of brandy every half hour, with camphor, etc., were faithfully

---

[1] China is located on the Rio San Juan about fifty miles from the Rio Grande.

administered, but all we knew and did was without avail, and at one o'clock he was gone. Poor fellow, he was kind to his companions, cheerful at his work, and twenty-four hours previously, was, to all appearance, perfectly well, and playing a game of whist with his brother and uncle.

For the last six or eight hours of his illness all the camp seemed to keep aloof from him, and all the tents on that side of the camp were deserted except Simson's and Harrison's, and those I ordered off. When Hinckley, Liscomb and Walsh came back from Rio Grande City with his coffin, I had prepared him for burial, for his brother was too prostrated with grief to do anything.

At five o'clock fifty of us followed him to the grave. As we thought he would have wished, and knew his friends would prefer, we buried him on the American side, in the grave-yard back of Davis' Rancho. Sadly we walked back with a feeling that this might not be the only case of the dread disease.

No time, however, was left for thought; as soon as I entered the camp Lambert's messmates came to beg me not to put them again in his tent. I told them I had no idea of doing so, gave them a new tent, struck his, levelled the ditches around it, and burned the withered boughs that had been put to shelter it. This done I went to rest if I could, being on this night of March 15th more anxious than I had been for years. I had just dropped into a troubled sleep, when I was called to look at Boden, one of the most athletic, regular men we had, who complained of great weakness and nausea. We had, of course, talked over Lambert's case, and as men will always try to assign causes for everything, whether they understand matters or not, we had said Lambert was always delicate and had overworked himself, but, here was Boden, a most robust, well-formed man, who had not exposed himself in any way to illness, and so we tried not to fear for him, but morning, March 16th, found him too weak to stand, and he showed signs of all the horrors of this dreadful disease. His broad forehead was marked with the blue and purple streaks of coagulated blood, and down both sides of the nose and blackening his whole neck the veins and arteries told that it was all over with him. "What hurts you, Ham?" I asked, as I saw distress in his face. "My wife and children hurt me, Mr. John," was his answer, which sent a thrill to my heart; I, too, had wife and children. I said what I could to console him, poor enough, doubtless, but from my heart, God knows, and with tears in my eyes, turned away to go to attend to Liscomb and Whittlesey, both just taken.

I gave proper directions and at Dr. Trask's suggestion went to Col. Webb's tent to tell him we must strike tents and leave the place at once. I met with a decided refusal at first, but on my repeating my request and stating the facts for a second time, he consented. The company was called and told that as previously arranged Col. Webb was going on to China to purchase mules, and that I was in charge of the camp, and would at once make arrangements to remove all the men who were well.

Providence here sent the steamer "Tom McKenny" passing on her way to Roma. I went on board and made the agreement that for one hundred dollars all who could go should be taken to Roma, and we at once set to work to pack and hurry everything on board, retaining only what I thought necessary for the three, now dying, men I had with me. I called for volunteers who responded instantly, and more than were needed, to remain with me; those who were finally decided upon for the sad duties before us, were Robert Simson, Howard Bakewell, W. H. Harrison, Robert Benson, Leffert Benson, John Stevens, James Clement, Nicholas Walsh, Talman and Follen, with the two Bradys who were friends of Boden, A. T. Shipman, W. H. Liscomb and Justin Ely.

As Dr. Trask could be of no further use, we insisted on his going on board the boat, as Follen was with us and knows a great deal about medicine, though leaving home just before taking his degree as a physician, deprives him of a title. All arrangements being made, I only waited for the boat to come up, and in a few minutes I had the gratification of hearing her last bell, and seeing her push off from our miserable camp for Rio Grande City.

When the order was given to go on board and take all the luggage, many started with only their saddlebags, either in terror, or in apathy, from the effect of the air on their systems. Scarcely more than twenty men were willing to take provisions enough to feed on for even one day. David Hudson showed himself one of the most energetic and helpful and there were some twenty others, but I was too anxious and too hurried in directing and working as well, to notice any but the most faithful, and the most unfaithful.

I took Langdon Havens on board, never expecting to see him again, he looked pale, yellow, blue, black, all colors at once, the large blood vessels of the neck swollen and black, showing how rapidly the disease was gaining on him, and begged Trask to do all he could for him. Then I came ashore and saw the boat off, turned away and stood for a moment to draw a long breath and wipe my streaming face, the mercury was 99 degrees in the shade. I looked at the group of good men who had reluctantly left me and had assembled in the

stern of the boat to bid me good-bye; in silence
they took off their hats, not a sound was heard but
the escapement of the steam   Sorrow filled my
heart for the probable fate of so fine a body of men,
but it was no time now for reflections, I had three
dying men on my hands, and the business of the
camp to attend to.

I went to the sick tents; poor young Liscomb
worn out and heart broken sat leaning against the
tent where his father lay dying, looking as pallid
and exhausted as the sick man, and almost asleep;
I roused him and sent him to my tent to get some
rest. Edward Whittlesey was next, looking as if he
had been ill for months; his dog, a Newfoundland,
was walking about him, licking his hands and feet
and giving evidence of the greatest affection; from
time to time smelling his mouth for his breath,
but it was gone.

I slowly walked to Boden's tent but there was no
change from the stupor into which he had fallen;
and I sat down to wait, for what?   All exertions
had been made to save our brave men, and all had
failed.   Like sailors with masts and rudder gone,
wallowing in the trough of a storm-tossed ocean,
we had to await our fate, one of us only at a time
going from tent to tent of our dying companions
to note the hour of their last breath.

I suddenly thought I would try one more
resource, and I sent John Stevens to Dr. Campbell

at Camp Ringgold, requesting him to tell the Doctor, if he did not know who I was, that we were Americans, and demanded his assistance. It came, but alas, his prescriptions and remedies were just those we had been using, calomel as soon as possible, mustard externally, great friction, opium for the pain, and slight stimulants of camphor and brandy. John Stevens had just returned, when Howard Bakewell, [who] had been his quarter of an hour watching the sick, came into my tent, where I was lying on my blankets, exclaiming, "My God, boys, I've got it, Oh, what a cramp in my stomach, Oh, rub me, rub away."

Simson and Harrison took him in hand, and I read and re-read Dr. Campbell's directions which we followed implicitly, but all to no purpose; one short half hour found Howard insensible to pain or sorrow. He asked me to tell his mother he had died in the Christian faith she had taught him, and his friends that he had died at his duty, like a man. So went one of our days opposite Davis' rancho, on the never-to-be-forgotten Rio Grande.

At four o'clock, p. m., two of our small company were dead, and two were lying senseless, and I told the noble fellows, who, forgetting self, still struggled for the company's good, that we would stay no longer in that valley of death, but to make every preparation to leave, and so they did. I was able

to help them but little, for with what I had undergone the last fifty hours, and the terrible death of
my young cousin, Howard Bakewell, I was utterly
exhausted. Simson, Clement and John Stevens
went with me across the river to the town, and the
rest packed what was most valuable, and hired men
to guard the camp that night.

I lay on a bed in a small house belonging to Mr.
Phelps, listening and awaiting the arrival of the
bodies of Bakewell and Liscomb, who were
brought over under the direction of Harrison and
Simson, and in a sort of a dream I heard their
footsteps, sprang from the bed, and Bakewell was
laid upon it. I waited for the rest of the party
with my saddlebags containing the company's
money; that was all of value that I thought of, and
sometimes I wonder I thought of anything, I was
so weary. But Clement brought them and Liscomb too, and the latter was laid out in the same
room with poor Howard. We then all went to
Armstrong's hotel, Clement carrying my bags and
valuables, and arriving found two more of our
party down with cholera. Dr. Campbell came to
see us and did all in his power for the sick, and
indeed for all of us, and told us it would be unsafe
for us to keep our money bags, but to give them
to the bar-keeper telling him their value, and
promising to pay him well for his trouble in caring
for them.

To tell how that night was passed would be more than I can do; Nicholas Walsh and A. T. Shipman became worse; I sent at once for Dr. Campbell and he passed the night with us. The heavy trade-wind from the south-east sighed through the open windows of the long twenty-bedded room we were in, the deep moans of young Liscomb, who, dreaming, saw nothing but the horrors of his father's death, our own sad thoughts, and the sickness of Walsh and Shipman, and our anxiousness, and perhaps nervousness, chased sleep away.

Morning came, and our friends had to be buried, and when this sad duty was over, we asked for our money, and to our amazement were told it was gone, had been delivered to one of our men. This was untrue, and we sent at once to the landlord and demanded our money. He coldly answered, "I never saw you, gentlemen, when money is left in this house, it is generally given to my charge, and then I am responsible for it." It was useless to explain that we had been unable to see him before, and, at Dr. Campbell's suggestion, we took charge of the man to whom we had intrusted it, and sent for the magistrate who took the evidence for and against, and committed the man to trial. As there was no jail, or place of security in which to confine him, we chained him to a musquit stump, and stood guard over him forty-eight hours, assistance from the garrison of Fort Ringgold having been refused us by Major La Motte.

March 18th. Today Harrison died of cholera after about twelve hours sickness, and I lost his assistance, which had been most valuable, and for a time that of Simson, who was well nigh crazy at the death of his friend, and who was besides completely under the influence of cholera, having been in the air of the malady nearly a week. The next day he was up again, his strong constitution, and still stronger mind, aiding his recovery, and again I had his services, given with his whole heart.

Today we told White, the man we held prisoner, that we were so enraged that we intended to hang him that night, or have the money back. When the sun was about an hour high, he said if we would let him go, he would tell where he had hid the money; we promised that if he recovered the money he might get away. At dusk we went with him to find it, but his accomplice had been ahead of him; never shall I forget his tone of despair, when on removing some brush and briars by a large cactus he exclaimed, "My God, it's gone." Accustomed to the summary way of judging and executing delinquents in Texas, he thought our next move would be to hang him. He swore by his God, his Saviour, and all that men held sacred, that that was where he had left the money, and prayed to be let go. Not one of us doubted the truth of what he said *now*, but we took him back, and again secured him, and that night Simson and Horde arrested Hughes, whom we thought to be his accomplice, finding him in a gambling house surrounded by his cronies. He, too, was secured and ironed, and slept on the ground, waking up in the morning demanding his "bitters," and as impudent as ever.

This day, March 19th, Mr. Upshur, a gentleman acting as attorney and agent for Clay Davis at Rio Grande City, and who had shown the greatest sympathy and kindness to us in our troubles, and exerted himself to the utmost to help us, called me to him, led the way to his room, closed and locked the door. He then asked me if I could swear to my money if I saw it. I told him I could not, but described it as well as I could remember. He showed me three or four thousand dollars in gold coin of different nations, and asked me again if I could swear to it. I could not, though I fully believed it was ours. He looked in my face so closely, that for an instant I thought he doubted who and what I was; but I met his clear eye, with one as honest, and slowly he drew a piece of brown post-office paper from his pocket, and asked: "Is that your handwriting?" "No," was my answer, "but it is that of Mr. Hewes of New Orleans, it is his calculation of five hundred dollars in sovereigns and half eagles which Layton and Hewes placed in my charge, and now I can swear to my money if that paper was with what you have showed me." He told me he had always been satisfied it was mine, as he knew there was not such an amount as I had lost, in the settlement. He counted it twice, took my receipt, and as we went to Camp Ringgold to leave it with the Quartermaster, Lieut. Caldwell, who was always most kind, Mr. Upshur told me the manner in which this portion of our money had been regained.

Don Francisco, a Mexican, and father-in-law of Clay Davis, was sheriff for the time, as the cholera had taken off the regular officer of "Star County." Whether Don Francisco was taking a midnight walk to see the fate of the "Californians," or watching what others might be doing to them, we could never find out, but either he had followed White and Hughes until they separated, after which he could only watch one, which he did until the thief had buried his share, which the Don promptly removed; or else, with the wonderful power of trailing which Indians and Mexicans possess, on the fact of our loss being made known to him, he may have found and followed the tracks of the thieves, and on discovering the money thinking this was all, have given up any further search, until the trails were obliterated by the footsteps of others. I may add here, that Don Francisco generously refused any compensation for what he had recovered, saying we had suffered enough.

The "Tom McKinney" which had taken our party to Roma brought back eighteen or twenty of the men on the way back to New Orleans. At first I thought they had returned to be of some assistance, but judge of my disappointment when I learned the truth. The Bensons, Bradys, Barclay, Tallman, Follen, Cowden, Ely and others were determined to go home. The Bensons came to me and said they were sorry to leave me, but they found they were not fit for such a journey as they had undertaken; many of the others went with a simple "Good-bye," and some did not even come up the hill to see me, and among these were some of whom I did not expect it, Walker, especially, for I thought a good deal of him, and had entrusted him with the care of the sick on their way to Roma; he never sent me any reason for not bidding me good-bye, but I attributed it to the sudden news of Harrison's death.

Desolate, indeed, did I feel as I watched the boat start on her return trip taking some of my very best men, or those I had thought were such, and I realized how little one can judge from appearances or when all is going smoothly. I was now left with only Simson, Clement, John Stevens, Nic Walsh, Mitchell and Elmslie, with Shipman very ill. We were, however, encouraged by good reports of those at Roma, Langdon Havens was recovering, and out of fifty-two more or less ill, only two had died, though twenty were yet too weak to move.

Horde, Upshur and Simson were taking most vigorous measures to recover our stolen money, and we again had Hughes on trial. He swore falsely again and again, that he knew nothing of it. We stood guard on him until we were compelled to rejoin our party, having recovered only about three thousand five hundred dollars, and lost all my papers, receipts, accounts up to date, besides letters of credit and introduction. I walked down to Camp Ringgold to see if possibly I might have a letter from home by a steamer just arrived, and on the road met Lieut. Browning on his way to join our company. I introduced myself to him and appointed an hour to meet him at the hotel at Davis's rancho, and went on to Major La Motte's tent for letters. He was engaged when I arrived, and too weary to sit down, I stretched myself on the rushes he had for the floor of his tent and commenced a conversation with Captain McCown, on the subject of our troubles. He did not know me, and began by: "The Audubons are well known in their profession, but————." I interrupted him by telling him he was too hard on me at first sight, and he was a little confused, but his frank apology soon put us on a friendly footing.

On my return to Davis's rancho, I saw poor Dr. Kearney who had undertaken the medical charge of the party; and I heard of the lives he had saved, and hoped still to have his aid for our suffering company. But the fatigue he had undergone was too much for him, and the day following this he was no more. He was buried at Camp Ringgold, where he had been cared for by Dr. Campbell, and nursed by his cousin, John K. Rodgers, one of my friends, who was so debilitated that he was obliged to return north.

Having done all we could to recover our money we left for Mier, via Roma, at the hottest hour of the day, three o'clock, hoping to arrive before dark, but after two hours stopped for shade and rest, for the heat, owing to our debility, was insupportable; at dusk we went on and reached Roma about eleven at night.

Roma, named after General Roman of Texan celebrity, is situated on a sandstone bluff, perhaps a hundred feet high, but like all the rest of the country on this line, with no trees, only an interminable chaparral of musquit, cactus (of three species), an occasional aloe, maguay[1] and wild sage, at this season covered with its bluish-purple flower, almost as delicate as the light green of the leaf. With the exception of the large, coarse

---

[1] Maguey is the Spanish name for the century plant.

cactus, which ought to be called "giganteus," almost all the plants are small leaved; worst of all, every tree, shrub and plant is thorny to a degree no one can imagine until they have tried a thicket of "tear-blanket" or "cat's claw."   The distant view was exquisitely soft, hill and valley stretching for miles about us, looking like a most beautifully cultivated country, the bare spots only like small fields, and the rest deluding the weary traveller in the belief that the distance is a change from the arid, bleak country through which he is riding.

We turned in at a small store, found a loaf of bread and some whiskey, and lay down on the floor with our saddles for pillows, and blankets for beds, and slept soundly.   At daylight I made up our party, saw them over the river in a small flatboat and rode on, thinking of our situation and wondering again and again how I could have been so thoughtless as to entrust our money to anyone, even with Dr. Campbell's advice, and what course to take now.   I could, of course, do nothing but await my interview with Col. Webb, who had written to bring the prisoners along and *he* would get the money.   The difficulty was that by the laws of Texas a man can not be taken out of his own county to be tried, and it is also against the law to lynch him.   Then, too, five men could not easily remove a desperado with some twenty accomplices, through twenty-five miles of wilderness.

I was so weak I was but just able to continue to ride, and so depressed in spirits that I was almost in despair.   We reached our camp on the Alamo River, a little creek three miles from Mier, and I was surprised to see a carriage as we rode up.   In a minute I saw Col. Webb sitting in it with one foot on the back seat and Dr. Trask bathing it.   He had had a touch of diarrhœa and had hired a carriage to ride down from S——— where he had received my letter advising him of our loss, and jumping out of the conveyance hastily, had sprained his ancle and was in great pain.   I found all in disorder, and the men came flocking round me, and, as I told them our experiences since I had written, they, in return told me of their own adventures.

Tonight, March 21st, Col. Webb was taken very ill with bilious cholera, and we thought he would have died; we worked over him until morning when he was better.

March 22.   Cholera broke out again this morning, and I was a sufferer, but not to die of it, and was lying twelve hours after my attack resting, when I was called to see young Combs who had just been taken ill.   The night before Mr. Upshur had sent for me, and a small force, to aid in a guard he wanted over a man he thought had a portion of our money, and, as was my custom, I called for volunteers (a lesson I learned from Jack Hayes[1] when I was in Texas), and Combs was one of the first to come forward. He was so debilitated I refused to let him go, and it was quite a task, tired and ill as I was, to convince him, it was his strength, not his spirit I doubted. How glad he was now, that I had not allowed him to go. Alas, he had a longer journey before him. At ten next morning the fatal stupor came over him. His friend J. J. Bloomfield had been like a brother to him, untiring in his devotion, and when in a few hours Combs ceased to breathe Bloomfield almost collapsed himself. Of the entire company that started with us for California, at one time numbering ninety-eight, Hudson, Bloomfield, Bachman and Damon were all who were able to help me perform the last rites for their companion.

After two hours hard work we had dug a grave, and returned to camp, the soil was a lime-like one, so hard that every inch had to be picked. Our whole camp was silent, as we wrapped Combs in his blankets; "not a drum was heard nor a funeral note," came strongly to my mind, and about twenty of the company started to follow to the grave; the burning heat of the day was past and the sun was just setting in a sky without a cloud. All

---

[1] Col. John C. Hays, the Texas ranger and Indian fighter, who won a national reputation at the siege of Monterey. He went to California in 1849, became first sheriff of San Francisco and afterward United States surveyor-general for California.

moisture seemed to have left the face of nature,
the distant prairies, broken only here and there by
a musquit, gave a wild desolation to the scene,
and as we fell into line without an order being
given, I thought I had never seen a more forlorn,
haggard set of men. Sadly indeed, did we bear
our late companion to his last home, and when we
reached the grave only eleven men had had
strength to follow. We lowered the body with
our lariats and I read the funeral service. As I
said, "Let us pray," all kneeled, and when I added
a short but heartfelt prayer for courage, energy
and a return of health to our ill-fated company,
not a dry eye was amongst us; not one man but
felt our position one of solemnity seldom, if ever,
experienced before by any of us. We returned to
our desolate camp to look on others still in danger
and needing consolation, even if we could not give
relief. So ended our last day on the banks of the
Alamo, and we retired to our tents to think on who
might be the next to go, all ideas of business being
for the time driven from our minds; even those
not ill, seemed almost apathetic.

March 23d. Again came morning with its
fiery sun burning and drying everything. Breakfast was tasted, but not eaten. A committee from
the company came to know what should be done.
Col. Webb with one of our doctors and four men
went off to Mier, to get out of the sun, for with all

his boast of, "I live as my men live," he said he "should die in that sun." I was obliged to go back to Rio Grande City about our money, so I told the men that we had better wait and see what further money we could recover and how our health was likely to be. All acquiesced, and with Clement and Simson I left for Roma on my way to Rio Grande, where I recovered four thousand dollars more of our money; I still hoped to regain the balance, about seven thousand dollars, but it was never found.

To tell of the dull monotony of this place would be most tedious, nearly as hard to think of as to endure. I found the officers of the camp my most sympathetic companions, Captain McCown, Dr. Campbell, Lieuts. Caldwell, Hazzard and Hayne, and Captain Deas.

Four days of fruitless examinations passed, and one night I had made my blankets into a bed, and was trying to find a soft position for my weak and bony legs, when Clement came to tell me I was wanted in Judge Stakes's room; with Lieut. Browning I went over. At a circular table covered with books and papers, lighted by a single candle, sat Clay Davis, his fine half-Roman, half-Grecian head resting on his small, well shaped hand, his position that which gave us the full beauty first of his profile, then of full face; his long black hair with a soft wave in it gave wildness and his black moustache added to a slight sneer as he looked at a Mexican thief standing before him; he was altogether one of the most striking figures I have ever seen. Opposite was Judge Stakes, also a very handsome man, as fair in hair and complexion as Clay Davis was dark. Behind him stood Simson with his Vandyke head and peaked beard; he was in deep shadow, with arms folded, and head a little bowed, but his searching eyes fixed keenly on the prisoner.

One step in advance stood Don Francisco putting question after question to the thief, a little further off stood three other rascals, their muscular arms tied, waiting "adjudication."

On the other side, in the light, sat another Mexican holding the stolen property which had been recovered; and behind him a table with glasses, bottles and a demijohn. Lieut. Browning and I sat on a cot bed covered with a Mexican blanket, watching the whole scene, denials, confessions, accusations, threats, and one after another piece by piece was produced of our property. All the clothes were recovered, amid questions and oaths in Spanish and English, until we abandoned all hope of regaining anything more.

With Lieut. Browning I left to return to Mier, but half-way between Davis's rancho and Roma met the company in wàgons which they had hired. All were well, but so weary and debilitated they

had decided to go home. I continued on my way
to see Col. Webb and get his ideas on the course
to be pursued. I received his orders and left at
two o'clock that night with his son, Mitchell, and
Lieut. Browning; regained the company, called
the men together, read their agreement to them,
and said all I could to remind them of the obliga-
tions they were under to go on and fulfil their
contract, but almost universal refusal met my
appeal. Only twenty-one agreed to go on; what
a falling off from ninety-eight! Out of those who
agreed to go on two were cooks, two teamsters,
two servants, and some few who said they did not
care for the company, they only wanted to go to
California. Can it be wondered at that I doubted
such men? I left them all to reconsider their
position, and went off to think over my own
troubles, and make up my mind how to act. In
half an hour I returned and told the men my
determination. "I have thought of my position
in the company, I have done all I could in the
interests of the company, but now I am going home.
I am not old enough to preach to you, but should
you go home, let contentment and gratitude for
what you have be gained by the hardships and
sorrows you have endured, and may God bless
those who go on, and those who return." So ended
"Col. Webb's California Co."

Fortune, always fickle, now changed. No

steamer came to take us back; for two days we were quite determined to take the voyage homewards, but with returning health the men began to feel encouraged, and I thought perhaps I ought to make another effort to go on. I consulted all I could on the subject, and of course had varying opinions. Captain McCown said: "Go back, no one can do anything with volunteers, you have no power to compel obedience; now you go back honorably, and you don't know what you will have to endure on a march through Mexico." Lieut. Caldwell urged me to go on, said "it was military education never to give up, so long as there was any possibility of the original idea being carried out."

Slowly I walked along thinking. I had not found the men disobedient, and I believed the cholera was the chief cause of discouragement, and the fact that Col. Webb had left the men in their distress the source of the anger against him. I decided that I could go on, and determined to make one more effort. That evening while sitting under an ebony tree, about eight o'clock, in the darkness which follows so rapidly on the short southern twilight, I heard a song from one of our company, and in a few minutes a chorus, good spirits seem to have returned, and leaving my seat I went over to Armstrong's Hotel.

On the counter of the bar-room lay Lieut.

Browning; two or three persons were seated at his feet, and on stools around the room lounged, or sat, our little band, our saddles, blankets, etc, filling a corner of the room. General Porter was there listening to the close of a chorus. One of the party pushed a saddle over for me to sit on, and I began my little address: "How strange it is that the thought of home should, in one short day, so change your spirits; who would have thought that fifty such men would be turned back by the first difficulties? What will you say to your friends? Forget your homes for a time and go on like men." But the old answer came, "We won't go on under the present management," and "We won't go on with Col. Webb." I told them it was not possible for them to go on with Col. Webb, as an hour before I had received a communication from him saying his health would not permit him to go on with us, and appointing a time to have a business interview with him before he left on his return home. A silence followed this announcement, and then Lieut. Browning said "Let's go on with Mr. Audubon." Three cheers gave their answer, but I told the men not to decide then in a moment of excitement, to wait until morning and make up their minds in cool blood, as I wanted no more change, and this would be their last resolve. At ten next morning we met, and all but six agreed to go on, and we at once moved to a camping ground five miles back from the Rio Grande, out of the way of cholera, to feed up our weak, and make our arrangements to leave. I at once ordered from Alexander sixty mules, thirty to be first-class saddle mules, and thirty good, average pack mules.

It took nearly a month to make all our preparations, wind up our business with Col. Webb and others, and to put our sick men in good travelling condition. When we had removed our provisions from Camp Ringgold, where we had stored them, our heaviest work was done, and we started for Mier, but found we had not mules enough and stopped at ——— to get more, and here we also repaired the miserable wagons that had been bought at Cincinnati, arranging our guard and other matters. Henry Mallory and I counted our money, and allowed a hundred days as the time requisite for our journey, and our financial calculations gave sixty-six dollars and four cents for each man.

How the responsibility of taking forty-eight men, most of them wholly ignorant of the life before us, through so strange and wild a country, weighed upon me, I cannot express, but we were too busy to have much time to think, and moved on twenty miles to Mier. Luckily our wagons broke down again, so we concluded to leave them, and lost another week disposing of them, and selling goods we were unable to take. At Mier I saw

Col. Webb off, with his proportion of money and provisions.

Mier is like every other Mexican town I have seen, it is composed of one square only, and all the rest suburbs, the houses built of adobe. To the southwest, hills, parched and arid, give an unpleasing foreground of the superb view of the mountains of Cerralvo, all the blue of Italy was again before me, with the exception of the blues of the Mediterranean Sea.

Two more of our company returned to us here, one of whom, Ulysses Doubleday, was so weak and reduced that I left him in charge of his friends Bachman and Elmslie, and gave him what money he needed to carry him home. I certainly thought him a dying man, but it was otherwise ordained, and he reached his friends safely and well. Bachman and Elmslie were true to me throughout all.

CHAPTER III

April 28th, 1849. The company started today, and I expect to follow early tomorrow, and join the men who are now fifteen miles ahead of me. I am compelled to remain to attend to the property of the ten men who have died of cholera in this accursed place; it goes to New Orleans by boat in the morning. Why Col. Webb, who had been in this country before, selected this route instead of a more northerly one, I cannot understand, but it is now too late to change, and we must go forward with courage.

April 29th. Canales Run. We are all on our way, having come to Ceralvo, [Cerralvo][1] beautiful for its old mission, and curious in its irrigating canals, bridges and old church, still it has the apathetic lassitude of everything Mexican. We rode on to Robber's Rancho, over undulating

---

[1] The route from the Rio Grande to the Rio Florida is described in Wislizenus's "Tour to Northern Mexico," Washington, 1848 (Senate misc. doc. 26, 1st session, 30th Congress) and in Bartlett's *Personal Narrative of Explorations and Incidents in Texas, New Mexico, California, Sonora and Chihuahua* (New York, 1854). Wislizenus was physician in Doniphan's expedition, and Bartlett was United States Mexican Boundary Commissioner. The Mexican Atlas of Garcia y Cubas (Mexico City, 1859) furnishes maps that are nearly contemporary and a list of haciendas.

wastes of hard, unprofitable soil. The palmettos are here by the thousand, and their fantastic shapes gave the appearance of horsemen of gigantic size, riding through grass almost as tall.

May 1st. Robber's Rancho, once a fine hacienda, was burned by the Americans, in the last war, for the rascality of its owners; it is on a beautiful plain, but brush has grown up in the now neglected fields, and all is in ruins. Here we came near losing Lieut. Browning from cholera, but he was saved by Dr. Trask's indefatigable exertions.

May 12th. Near Monterey. We have been here four days having horses and mules shod, and I will take my pencil notes and write up my journal to date.

We were at Robber's Rancho a week, waiting for Bachman, Elmslie and Carrol, who had been left with Doubleday. As soon as they rejoined us we moved on to Papogias [Popagallos] then to Ramos where we met some French traders with a long train of mules and their "cargoes."

Ramos was followed by Marin and Aquafrio; all present a dilapidated appearance, very different from what was seen when the country was under the fine system of irrigation, and the remains of past opulence everywhere sadden the traveller.

We reached Walnut Springs, five miles from Monterey, on the 8th of May, and are taking needed rest in the shade of the Spanish walnuts, and enjoying the delightful water, which bursts out in a fountain of six to eight feet wide, and about a foot deep, clear but not cool, yet pleasant to drink. Monterey is at the base of a range of mountains, which surround it on all sides except to the north. Its entrance over bridges, many of them very picturesque, shows abundance of water, which irrigates the beautiful valley for miles beyond Molino.

Where did I hope to be at this date? Yet here we are scarcely started; one month lost in sickness and sorrow, and one in the re-organization of our company. We are full two months behind our reckoning, and on a route of which I never approved, but which, when I took command, we were already compelled to pursue. We are having the horses and mules shod, for their feet are so tender we can not continue without. We travel, usually twenty or twenty-five miles a day, as the chance for water and forage for our horses occurs. The uncertainty of provisions is such that we have to carry corn for one or two feeds ahead, which adds considerably to the weight of our packs, and gives us a good deal of trouble.

As I sit here, I hear the notes of many new birds, as well as those well known, and the sky overhead is bluer than any Italy ever presented to me. Monterey, where I have been several times, is an improvement on the other Mexican towns we visited, but full of foreigners of all nations come to prey on the ignorance of the poor inhabitants. All now seems well regulated, but I dread shortness of provisions and we have to be very careful. I have not heard from home since the date of February 19th and now must wait, I fear, until we reach, if we ever do reach, the Pacific coast.

The company are all tired, the work is new and it takes time to become accustomed to the broken night's rest. At midnight I take the rounds of our camp in moonlight, starlight or darkness, to see that all is well, and that none relax in vigilance, so requisite to safety in this country of thieves. This gives me only six hours of sleep, for after we have had supper, it is eight o'clock, and we get up at four a. m., so that taking out the two hours nightly, reduces me to that amount, but "habit is second nature." If you hear of any more men coming to California overland, tell them three shirts, six pairs of socks, one coat, one great coat, two pairs of trousers and two pairs of boots, should be all the personal luggage. No man should bring more than he can carry.

I have had quite a scene with the Alcalde here. Our camp was infested with pigs, which came from every direction every morning and evening when we fed our horses and mules. Of course, we could not see them robbed, stones and hatchets were abundant, and some pistols went off, which the boys declared did so accidentally. We could not find the owners, so I went to [the] Alcalde to pay for them, taking an Italian boy as interpreter. The boy instead of saying what I told him, which was simply to ask the value and pay it, added on his own account, that if his Honor was not satisfied with what we gave, we would come in and take the town. Naturally the Alcalde resented this, and I found my little vagabond had been telling his own story, not mine. Upon matters being explained by a more trustworthy source, the Alcalde was perfectly content, and bowed me out with much courtesy.

The adroitness of the Mexicans in thieving equals that of the rascals at Naples. In two instances pistols have been taken from the holsters whilst the owners held the bridles of their horses. All this has tended to excite revenge, and without good discipline outbreaks of temper might have occurred, which would undoubtedly have brought us into trouble, as happened with several other companies on the road to Mazatlan.

Saltillo, May 20th. Here we are, thank God, fairly on our way, and at present in good health and spirits. We travel about twenty-five miles a day, but have great difficulty in keeping our horses and mules in good order, as there is no grass for grazing purposes, and corn varying in quality, but always high in price, from one dollar to fifty cents per bushel.

When we left Monterey we followed the road to Rinconada, which is a beautifully located rancho, well watered and with a long avenue of pollard poplars or cotton-woods; the boles not more than ten or fifteen feet high, so that the flawy gusts that are like little hurricanes for a few seconds, and which come from the mountains which surround the place in every direction, cannot blow them down. Here we saw the first magua plants, from the juice of which pulke [pulque] is made, and afterwards muscale [mescal] distilled. Muscale in taste is more like creosote and water, slightly sweetened, than anything I can compare it to, and I suppose it is about as wholesome.

The peons who do the work of the hacienda are completely Indian in character, appearance and habits, sometimes marvelous in their strength and activity, and sometimes surprising us with their unsurpassed laziness. The women, patient things, like all squaws, carry wood, water, and do all the household labor.

From this beautiful little amphitheatre among the hills we wound along parched arroyos and valleys, and I could not but be struck with the wise provision of nature for the protection of its creations. Almost all the trees have tap roots, or if fibrous, they run so deep in search of moisture, that they are often longer than the tree is high. In the arroyos where the earth was often washed from the roots, I had a good opportunity of confirming my conclusions. We proceeded up a deep ravine, until we began the ascent of the famed pass of Rinconada, intended to be defended by Santa Anna, but abandoned when our troops approached. How any force of artillery could have deserted such a position I can not conceive, for the unfinished fort commands the road for two miles at least.

The view from the Fort was most superb, but we were tired of mountains, and longed for shade and woods. Crossing this pass we had our first indication of increasing altitude, and above us on the rocks were pines and cedars. They had the showers we longed for and saw passing, while almost smothered in dust, our hair and whiskers white with it, and we looked like a troop of grey veterans.

We approached Saltillo over a broad plain, dotted with ranchos for some miles before we reached the town, which we entered through lanes of adobe walls, and finally came to the principal street, and commenced the ascent of the hill on which the town proper stands. It is all Mexican in its character, one story houses, flat roofed and having a fortified look, as if no one trusted his

neighbor. The public square is a fine one, and
the cathedral front the most beautiful I have seen
on this side of the Atlantic. The workmen who
did the carving came from Spain, and the stone
from the Rocky Mountains, so goes the story.
Saltillo has many good points, it is clean, well
regulated, and [has] better buildings than any I
have seen except at Monterey, yet we pushed on,
and have made our camp at Buena Vista, six miles
further on. High mountains bound our view on
every side. Buena Vista had its battle, and few
of us but have some friend or acquaintance sleep-
ing there.

Parras, May 28th. I shall never forget the
Buena Vista Camp, the night of the 23d and 24th,
it was the night previous to our departure for this
place; the guard was slow in coming out, Montrose
Graham was guard over my tent that watch, and
as Simson called his guard to order, and faced me,
where I had risen up to see who were changing,
George Weed let his rifle fall. The cock was
down on the nipple, contrary to a positive order;
in falling, the head of the hammer struck the
ground first, and, as if the trigger had been pulled,
it went off. An exclamation came from either
side, one "Mr. Audubon's killed," the other from
me: "Who's hurt?" A groan from poor Graham
was the answer. We were all hurry for lights
and water, and the Doctor. All loved Graham,

he was the handsome man of the original party of ninety-eight, just twenty-two, and the Captain of his tent, "The Hailstorm Mess," so called by Lieut. Browning, from its go-ahead principles.

The ball had passed through his ancle, and both Drs. Perry and Trask said he could not go on for some weeks. So it was decided to leave his cousin, Molinear, with him, a more practical physician than most of his age, and as much money as we could spare, that they could follow us or return home, as seemed most judicious.

Frank Carrol, as good a man as I ever wish on such an expedition, found accommodations for Graham, and remained with him at Saltillo. How we parted from them only those can know who have been compelled to leave friends in a strange land.

For several days our road continued over long hills, and parched valleys, and on the last day of this travel we had a most extraordinary view. We had climbed a hill, not more than three hundred feet high, but very steep, and reached a broad plain five or six miles wide, but much longer. On every side was a chain of sterile volcanic mountains; it was, for one view, most wonderful; it looked as if an immense lake, that threatened to cover the mountains, had suddenly been changed to earth. Crossing this plain and rounding one of the desolate peaks, we came to the hacienda of Don

Emanuel Hivarez, who has five hundred peons at work. The water used for irrigation, without which nothing could be grown, is brought in an adobe aqueduct for several miles. It is an old settlement and very dirty, abounding in fleas and vermin of all descriptions. Yet when one comes to a hacienda with water all round, brought from some mountain stream, the contrast between the desolate land we have travelled and the exuberant luxuriance of vines, figs and magua gives a beauty which almost makes me, with my hatred of everything Mexican, admire our surroundings. Mocking-birds are all around us, and could I linger to explore, I have no doubt I could have added many new birds to my list, but with cholera hanging round, breaking out, in a mild form it is true, at every place we stop at, we must push on.

We daily pass cacti of three species, as well as miles of aloes, yet not enough nourishment to feed a horse in the whole of them, and through this country we start tomorrow for Chihuahua. We have one hundred and fifty-seven mules and horses and fifty-seven men, and are in good spirits. We hear Chihuahua is our best route, but we may have different information at Parral and go through Sonora.

May 29th. Parras is like all Mexican towns I have seen, a few French and Americans, some with a Mexican wife, others with a housekeeper;

but all indolent, keeping little stores and warehouses and making immense profits. It is celebrated for wines and brandy, made principally by foreigners.

May 30th. At three o'clock this morning I was taken with sharp pains, nausea and other symptoms of cholera, and for the first time was obliged to ride in the ambulance, but towards evening was able to be up again, though very much debilitated.

June 2d. We left Parras at five this morning, and at dusk reached El Paso [El Pozo], and camped on a gravelly hill. For miles a barren desert lined both sides of our road, until we came to a swamp tract, with extraordinary luxuriance of rank weeds, no grass, and passing this entered a dismal thicket of chaparral.

June 3d, Sunday. We left El Paso at eight this morning, and rode until ten, when we reached a deserted rancho, and with some trouble encamped near a river bed with waterholes along it. A beautiful lagoon with water holes a hundred yards long enabled us all to take refreshing baths, and I watched with pleasure the languid flight of the great blue heron, changing his position as he was approached. Two Mexicans, hunting cattle, came to us here, and Lieut. Browning bought a wild mule, for which he gave a few dollars and a broken down mule.

June 2d. [?] Again we have been through swamp-like country, crossed the dry bed of a river, with white sand glaring painfully in our faces, and found acres of wild sunflowers, and patches of what looked like horehound, then we came to a cotton-wood bottom, gradually changing to a golden willow, which grew so luxuriantly on both sides of the road that I was reminded of the rich bottom lands of Ohio.

At noon we came to Alamito, a large rancho, or small village of scoundrels. In bargaining for water, which is only to be had from wells, we found the men who had it for sale were making their own terms with our rascally guide, and Simson stepped up and began talking to them. They pretended they could not understand, but on my tapping my revolver they instantly became most intelligent.

Here we had the first attempt at a "stampede" made upon us. Those intending to run off the "cabalgada"[1] of a travelling party, take a strong horse, cover him with the skin of an ox which has been newly killed, putting the fleshy side out, tie all the bells they have to the horse, and fastening an enormous bunch of dry brush to his tail, set fire to it, and start him off with yells and shouts through

---

[1] *Cabalgada* is properly a troop of mounted men or cavalcade. The word is here applied to the animals upon which the men are mounted.

the camp of those to be stampeded. Horses and mules, keen of scent and hearing, receive warnings of danger through both faculties, and are so frightened they will break any ordinary fastening. No matter which way they go, the vagabonds are such beautiful riders they soon turn the herd to any course they like, and make their escape, for those robbed have nothing to follow on; for, even if a few animals are left, the speed of the thieves can never be equalled. In this instance our vigilant guard saved us; what would have become of us if they had not, I dare not think.

June 7th, Mapimi. After a ride of twenty leagues we reached this place last night just before twelve, and lay down without food for either ourselves or our horses, and the poor animals had only had water once that day. The journey had been well enough. From time to time we enjoyed a pleasant shade through a larger growth of musquits than common, and again the country was bare of all vegetation. Tired though we were, our sleep was poor, for we were in a sort of barnyard full of hogs, and surrounded by thieving Mexicans.

This is a mining town and has several smelting furnaces where charcoal is used. Lead, and about an ounce of silver to every hundred pounds of ore, is produced, so the silver pays for the smelting, and in some of the mines copper is found. The furnaces externally are picturesque, not high, but with eccentric peaks, mitre-shaped, and harmonizing well with the rugged mountains which surround this dirty little town, where idleness and dirt, dogs and fleas abound.

June 9th. We rested a day at Mapimi, and reached La Cadena this evening, having come nine leagues; we shall stay here tomorrow to have the tires of our wagon set and to rest. This rancho has a fortified appearance, and mounts one small cannon, it looks able to resist a heavy attack from the Indians.

The road to this place is almost level for twenty miles, when, entering a gorge with abundant grass, it winds up a gradual ascent for two or three miles, and to the west we had a grand view, in the middle of which stood the hacienda. A long front of white wall, a tower at each end, with the usual archway in the center, over which was mounted a small brass piece, made the whole show of the establishment; and though formidable to the Apaches, who are about here in numbers, to us was only picturesque. Today we lost two of our best horses with cholera; the poor beasts suffering so much in the manner that men do, that it was painful to have our own troubles brought back so forcibly to our minds.

June 10th. We left for Pantilla at eight last night; it was eleven leagues distant; and being a deserted rancho no food could be had there, so we intended watering at the place, taking a short rest, then going seven leagues farther to La Zarca. Two hours after we started the moon rose behind us, and truly we presented a most picturesque appearance. Some in coats, some in blankets Mexican fashion, others in shooting jackets; we grew very tired and longed for sleep, but it was not to be taken except on horseback. Morning came and we stopped for an hour to graze our horses and mules, and rode past the deserted rancho without stopping to water, and came on to La Zarca, having had our poor animals under the saddle for twenty hours, during which we made sixty-four miles, ourselves only having to eat what we had expected for one meal. As we came up the mountains that overlooked this plain, we saw the first antelopes, and I was at one time within two hundred yards of three, but I did not shoot, and was never so near again. Many black-tailed hare have been seen and shot, and their variety of pelage would make twenty species.

June 12th. Today, Sunday, we are resting men and animals, and tranquillity is all about us. These long journeys are very injurious to our horses; one such long trip leaves them much more jaded and impoverished than two shorter ones, even though, as now, we always take a day's rest.

La Zarca is beautiful to look at, the centre of attraction being a fine clump of cotton-woods, letting the white walls of the hacienda shine

through them.   We bought a beef, killed it, and
our meal was speedily cooked and eaten.   Looking
day after day on the same desolate scene, rendered
so only by the want of rain, rarely camped in
shade, this journey becomes wearisome beyond
belief.

The broad plain on which this rancho is situated
once grazed six thousand head of horse, all owned
by one person, but when the Spanish government
was given up for no government, which is the case
now, Indians and Mexicans supplied themselves
with stolen horses in abundance.

June 13th.   From La Zarca to Cerro Gordo the
country is flat and uninteresting, barren in most
places of all but musquit bushes.   Every mile or
so for the first few leagues we crossed a beautiful
little brook, which was, however, gradually
absorbed by the thirsty sand, a water hole and bed
of sand appearing alternately, until the water
wholly disappeared.   We made two days' journey
of it, going the first day eighteen miles, where we
found good grazing on partially dry grass, better
for horses and mules than corn alone, which half
the time has been all we could get for them.   Our
most serious trouble now is the sore backs of our
mules produced by the pack saddles, which were
made in our own country, and are too broad for
the backs of the Mexican mules.   Cerro Gordo is
a miserable den of vagabonds, with nothing to

support it but its petty garrison of a hundred and
fifty cavalry mounted on mules. We were hooted
and shouted at as we passed through, and called
"Gringoes," etc., but that did not prevent us from
enjoying their delicious spring water; it was cool
and delightful. Our men rushed to it, and drank
two pint cups full each, hardly breathing between
times; it was the first good water we had had since
leaving the Mississippi.

Here we were visited by a member of a Mexican
travelling circus, who asked our protection as far
as El Valle, which we promised them. The party
consisted of five, one woman and four men. The
lady rode as we used to say in Louisiana "leg of a
side," on a small pacing pony; the two horses of
the ring carried only their saddles, two pack mules,
four small trunks, and four jaded horses the rest
of the plunder. The four men went one on foot,
driving the packs and continually refitting and
repacking, the other three riding. One man had
two Chihuahua dogs about six inches long, stuffed
in his shirt bosom, another a size larger on the
pommel of his saddle. A second man was in
grand Spanish costume, on a small but blooded
grey horse, with a large dragoon sword on his left,
and a Mexican musket made about 1700, which
would have added to an antiquary's armory. They
told us they had everything they owned with them,
so that if alone, and attacked by the Apaches, whom

we hear of continually but never see, their loss would be a very serious one to them.

June 14th. We left Cerro Gordo at eight a. m. and ascended steadily up hill for about two miles, the country poor and uninteresting, and the miles seem to stretch out interminably. We are now camped at El Noria.

June 15th. Rio Florida. We are repaid for our tiresome journey by the shade and refreshment we find here; the old mission is the most commodious we have seen, built of nearly white marble, the four pillars next the church richly carved and almost perfect. When the old priests had this broad valley tilled and irrigated by the convert Indians it must indeed have been a scene of luxurious growth, and they, no doubt, lived in great comfort, if isolation. Still the place is inland, and indolence there as everywhere in Mexico reigns supreme. So fell Rio Florida.

June 17th. From Rio Florida to El Valle, ten leagues, our road in places has been most beautiful; undulating plains like those of Texas, and we saw the first streaks of iron mixed with the limestone which for weeks we have been traveling through. We shall be glad of any change, for our lips are cracked, and so sore as to give pain and discomfort all the time, while our hands are cracked and split as in mid-winter.

Here at El Valle, sometimes called Bia Valle,

we are encamped in a grove of cotton-wood, which, I should say, had been planted forty or fifty years ago, and the gardens when irrigated must have been most luxuriant. We are now in an iron district, and the walls of the Jacals have changed from white to red. The hillsides, too, have changed in color; some are reddish and bare, others grey, from dead grass and lime underneath.

Bia or El Valle is situated on another of those beautiful creeks that from time to time occur in this part of Mexico; it contains a motley crowd, doubtful of face and of character; largely half-breeds, and speaking Spanish, so murdered into patois, that Lieut. Browning, a fluent Spanish scholar, was some time learning to understand their language. Our circus party left us here; the woman who was really the queen of the show came to thank us for our protection, which she did most gracefully, and gave us a courteous invitation to her show and fandango, the termination to every Mexican entertainment, wedding, christening, and even battle. I could not go, but several of the party did, and pronounced the senoritas quite good looking.

June 18th, Parral.[1]   Half way between El Valle and Parral, at a rancho on one of the bends of the Rio Florida, is a most splendid specimen of

---

[1] Hidalgo del Parral, marked upon the maps both as Hidalgo and as Parral, but more commonly the latter.

meteoric iron, almost pure in quality. It is, at its
highest point, four feet above the ground, and
from two to five feet one way, by two to three the
other, very irregular. Where it is worn by the
passers by rubbing their hands it is bright, and
looks like a lump of pure ore.

A long, steep zigzag descent, rocky beyond
belief, and painful to our poor mules, many of
which had lost shoes, brought us into Parral, which
is wild and picturesque in situation as well as in
buildings, but yet desolate.

The balconies, so to speak, built in front of the
silver mines, high on the sides of the mountains
which entirely surround the town, give it a fortified
appearance, and convey the idea of a respectability
which we have not seen since we left Saltillo. We
skirted the town, and are encamped on the banks
of the river or creek that runs through the centre;
our tents were soon in place and guard set, for we
were immediately surrounded by at least a hundred idlers. While talking to some Americans,
Lieut. Browning had his pistol stolen from his
holster, while standing within three feet of his
mule. This makes the fifth lost in this way. He
drew his revolver and ordered the crowd off, and
in an instant the ground was clear, and the fear that
characterizes these miserable creatures was shown
as they hurried off, holding their hats to shield the
back of their heads.

We are, comparatively speaking, camped in a paradise, for we have pollarded cotton-woods to give us shade, a dashing little brook, and an aviary of birds to enliven or calm, to cheer and encourage us, and are in real enjoyment of rest from fatigue and pain, all but my thigh, which is very painful from the presence of a large boil.

June 20th. Parral. So far our prospects ahead are good, and we have determined not to take the Chihuahua route, but the mountain one from this to Jesus Maria, and so on, as we are informed from the best authorities that we can go that way without suffering from want of water or food, and arrive at the mouth of the Gila, not three hundred miles upstream. We are told of both routes by those who have personally travelled them, and learn that by taking to the mountains we shall be in pine forests, and that deer and bear are frequently found, so that we shall be able to have some variety from the monotonous fare of no meat or only tough beef, which we have had for three months.

All would have been well had we not encountered cholera, and lost that never-to-be-caught-up-with time at Davis's rancho; and no party would have beaten us over. We have passed the Comanche country, and now have to be on our guard against the Apaches. No one knows how constantly I miss my dear friend Dr. Kearney in times like these, especially when a deviation from our contemplated route is in question.

The country we have passed through is desolate in the extreme, parched, arid, barren, except where irrigated.

Parral is a mining town where silver is found, but there is no proper machinery for satisfactory work. There are about seven thousand inhabitants of the usual mixed variety.

June 27th, 1849. Here at Parral we have found some Americans, and, as ever, friends among them; Mr. Hicks and Mr. Miller in particular; but here unfortunately Hinckley, Liscomb and Teller were taken ill, and our departure was delayed. Teller was very ill from the first with a sort of cholera. We took him into the town for better accommodation and rest, but he sank rapidly; we were unable to save him, and could only alleviate his sufferings. His cousin and myself watched over him with heavy hearts, and depression again settled heavily on our camp.

CHAPTER IV

ACROSS THE MEXICAN MOUNTAINS TO ALTAR

June 28th. Left Parral at noon, leaving Carroll, E. A. Lambert, J. S. Lambert, J. Black, Penny-packer and Joseph Lambert to follow after burying poor Teller. Before this we had sold our Jersey wagon for $275.00 and I refused $250.00 for two mules, as I did not dare to start short handed in animals, their lives here are so uncertain. Our start was late, not only owing to the loss of our companion, but because the night previous we had a severe storm with thunder and lightning, which had drenched tents, blankets and men; many of the men were stiff and cold, and we had to dry the tents and blankets to save weight on our mules, but when we did start, we wound along a glen that led to our first view of the spurs of the eastern chain of the Rocky mountains, and exclamations of delight burst forth from all.

We rode until six this evening, twenty miles, when another terrific storm coming on, we camped on a grassy flat, among musquit and scrub oaks, with good feeding for horses, but bad water. It rained too hard to make a fire, so we dined on bread and Parral cheese, not bad I assure you. Each man was served with a tin cup of brandy and water. The question was brought up as to whether or not brandy was essential, except in real illness. As we sat in the dim light of our lantern, drenched and cold, we decided in the affirmative, and if our friends could have seen us, they would, I think, have sanctioned the vote.

At ten o'clock I turned myself and my guard out, and Henry Mallory and his twelve men were my relief; the guard being unusually large, thieves here being so numerous that guards must be close enough to see each other, even on a dark night.

June 29th. We passed through patches of beautiful scarlet lilies, that sometimes were an acre in extent, gorgeous and splendid, and contrasting with an equally abundant blue-flowering plant like larkspur, but alas, I am no botanist. We here came to the first great ascent we had made for some time. Had we not been told that La Zarca was the highest point in central Mexico, we should have thought ourselves a thousand feet higher than at any previous time on our trip. Up we went through scrub, post and live-oaks filled with mistletoe, and a most beautiful laurel, with the stems and branches bright cinnamon orange. At last we arrived at the top of the ridge, and came to a jutting point giving a view of the most magnificent mountain pass that can be imagined. Our men gave a shout for mere exultation, and I partook of their buoyant spirits, and cried out: "Three cheers for these glorious hills," and such cheers!! Echo after echo responded, and we gazed then in silence at the superb cliffs, volcanic, basaltic, and sandstone, all discolored with the iron prominent on the surface, and below us the beauties of a little torrent that dashed on to the west as fast as I could have wished to go.

Our course was downward now, and as we descended the forest grew taller; laurel, pine, oak, a wild cherry, a cedar, new to me, two feet six inches in diameter, with balls and foliage like arbor vitae, and bark furrowed like an ash, ornamented the beautiful gorge; besides there were the common cedar and many splendid walnut trees. To describe the road would be rather difficult; it was just passable, that is to say *could* be passed; in many places not easy work for our packs. Most of us led our horses, either to save them or ourselves, for a stumble might send us two or three hundred feet down, and was not to be risked.

Just as we reached the valley Maybury was taken ill with what resembled cholera, and could not ride on in the heat of the day, so Dr. Trask, Simson, Mallory and Pennpacker remained behind with him. The rest of us went on for ten miles, and encamped on a beautiful, rolling prairie under some post and narrow-leaved swamp oaks. It rained most violently as usual, as it has done every evening since we entered the mountains. Fortunately, before it began Maybury and the men left to care for him reached camp.

June 30th. A fine morning. As we had no fresh meat we took a little bacon, our never failing standby, and going on came to Huajatita, and camped two miles beyond. Here we bought a six-months-old calf for five dollars, and abundance of corn for two dollars and fifty cents per cargo (six bushels). I am so enchanted with the wild beauty all about us, that I could almost stay months to enjoy it. It is all new to me; the hills and mountains are different in shape from any I have seen; the plants, trees, rock, all strange, and as we take our horses to the beautiful creek to drink, curious fish come to look at their noses.

July 1st. Again our road was up hill, and most dangerous, so most of us walked, but with all our care nearly lost two mules, by mis-steps. The narrow passes are so worn by the trains of pack mules, that, to insure safe footing, each mule puts his foot in the same worn hole that other mules have trod, for, perhaps, fifty years previously. Two of our train failing to do this rolled over four or five times, and how they ever recovered their footing is a mystery; a horse under similar conditions would have gone to the bottom.

To us, so long suffering from drought and bad water, the showers that come daily in the afternoon about three o'clock, and the little streams we cross, are most enchanting. The ride today was very interesting.

July 2d. We are leaving the mountains and I dread the plains again, they are so monotonous. We found some wild grapes, and, to *us*, the most matured were not sour. Liscomb was taken ill today with dysentery, and we feared we should lose him. Tone put him on his horse, the easiest we had, and Carroll was most kind to him; we were compelled to go on, but we gave him short rests as frequently as we could.

Gradually the plain narrowed, and as we neared the ridge of mountains which bounds one side of the valley of Santa Cruz, we passed the ruins of a once beautiful Mission. It was a low, Gothic style of architecture, built of yellowish white sandstone.

We waited in the shade of the walls of Santa Cruz to rest young Liscomb, and the main company wound its way along to a rancho a few miles distant where we could get corn for the horses and mules. I did not have time to see enough of Santa Cruz to describe it. Like all the towns of this part of the country, it has the remains of strong walls, that fifty years ago gave safety from the incursions of the Indians.

As the day cooled we took Liscomb on, and crossed the Conchos River, called by the natives, of course, "Rio Grande," as they call every river in Mexico. On reaching camp I found Langdon Havens had killed three glossy ibises at one shot; they are most abundant here, also white egrets and green herons, and I was delighted to see buff-necked Cormorants of California, and many other birds strange and new, but no time have I to study them, or even to secure and prepare specimens, and how could I carry them if I had them?

I was called here to see Carroll, who while measuring corn was taken with a violent fit, after which he was so exhausted we had to leave him behind with four men, and we rode ten miles further on, and at the setting of the sun came to a little river, with high bluffs, and most beautiful in the light and shade given by the clouds.

Our path has been most precipitous, alternately descending and ascending, to and from the river. Never in any country have I seen more beautiful lands; we rode through groves of water-oak, and what I should call willow-oaks, with a sweet little acorn, almost as good as a nut, occasionally pines and cedars; and there are many little brooks, in nearly all of which are fish, so I presume there must be water holes all the year round.

Antelopes are seen from time to time, but only one or two a day, wonderfully scarce for a country apparently so well adapted for both deer and antelopes. The black-tailed hare is seen too, but scarce, compared to the numbers we saw after leaving Parras.

Leaving this place we rode along a sandy bottom, which in the rainy season is the bed of a torrent. We left just before sunrise, and the heavy dew of this country gave such a freshness to all vegetation that nature seemed more luxuriant than ever. The prairies at this season present to our view many beautiful flowers, nearly all of a most delicate character, like primroses, larkspurs, sweet williams. Nettles six feet high, their blue flowers almost hiding the rich green of their stinging leaves, extend, sometimes, for miles along the sand bars. The cactus seems to have been left behind. We now found quantities of mushrooms, looking like the same species at home, and having the same flavor both raw and cooked.

The minerals I cannot speak of, but Dr. Trask tells me that there is a good deal of silver, and some gold in the earth mixed with quantities of lead. The stone is sandstone, and now and then we see most beautiful marbles, black and white, in strata, as if laid by hand.

We killed three pigeons today, and have seen many, of what I take to be either Steller's Jay or the ultramarine, but they are so shy, we cannot get at them. One of "the boys" gave me two young marmots, but I cannot place them, though the spots are a good deal like the Mexican, but not regular enough for that species. The land snail, which as far as Monterey was abundant, has gradually disappeared, and we are now free from it. The eatables in this country are scarce, no vegetables except beans, onions, and a very small pea. Beans are seventy-five cents an "Almud." Corn one and one half to three dollars a "fanega" (nearly three bushels). Cattle, half grown, three to twelve dollars. Sheep from a dollar and a half to two dollars. Hogs, strange to say, run up to eighteen and twenty dollars, and are fattened expressly for the lard, which is as high as eight dollars for twenty five pounds, and a very large, fat animal has sold for fifty dollars.

Concepcion, about the twentieth town of the name we have passed, is a dirty little place, with a church and nunnery. The inhabitants are like all other Mexicans, and are in eternal dread of the Apaches. So far we have not seen a hostile Indian, and only once a trail, which was that of the "Taromari" [Taraumara][1] tribe, and our guide said were not Bravos. Many of the people take advantage of us as an escort, and run along either before or behind, and at night camp near us.

July 2d. We wound along the meanderings of the river "Verde," sometimes smooth and again a dashing torrent, and reached "El Rancho

---

[1] The Taraumara or more properly the Tarahumara Indians are described in H. H. Bancroft's *Native Races*, vol. i, chap. v.

Arisachi," deserted by its original owners. It is worked by Tarimari Indians and owned now by some one whose name we could not find out. We tried to buy cattle, for we had had no fresh meat for several days; but any we pointed out could not be bought, no owner could be found. I told Van Horn, our best shot, to pick out the fattest yearling he could find, and we would pay the owner if he came forward. The beast was no sooner shot than a man claimed the price. By the time we had dressed the animal, and packed the four quarters on our meat mules, no vestige was seen of the dead animal — entrails, head, etc., being carried off by the Indians.

From this rancho we had to leave our beautiful stream for a mountain pass, and the first precipice we ascended cost Watkinson his horse; the poor brute had no bones broken, but was so lame from his fall, that we had to leave him behind. There was plenty of grass and water in the valley near which he fell and we hoped he would be found and cared for, not eaten, as among these Indians is the rule when horses or mules are broken down or injured. In places our road was almost impassable, but we reached the top of the first hill and had a view of the next, about three times higher. We could see very distinctly the zig-zag line of our road, in the red clay between the rocks and stones, and foresaw hard work for ourselves and our animals. Down we went, and in half an hour after began the new ascent. We were compelled to leave a mule here, and to divide his pack between two or three other animals.

Soon after, we made the last ascent, most abrupt and trying of all, but from the summit had a magnificent view of a broad plain such as I have never seen surpassed. On either hand mountain after mountain covered with oak and pine, and contrasts of sun and shade were before us, and the velvety distance ended in a rainbow. After a heavy descent we encamped on the brink of a little creek, overhung by tall pines.

Here we saw two elks, and Jack Black, mounted on a tired mule thought he could get near enough to have a shot, but after going about two miles, changed his mind.

July 3d. This morning we started early, and our road along this little stream was beautiful and so quiet that I lagged behind to enjoy it as much as possible, but in a short time we began a stony ascent of two miles, after which came an uncomfortable descent into another beautiful valley, but with poor grass; here we took a short rest, and then continued, reaching, at noon, Tomochic, on a little river of the same name. The old Mission had only the original tower; the rest of the building is now adobe.

The river here makes a sudden turn from south-

east to northwest, and we took it up-stream; it
runs through miles of sandstone worn into cliffs
and fissures, presenting the most fantastic shapes
imaginable, delighting us at every turn.   We
looked in vain for fish in the most tempting of
eddies and holes, but saw very few; little trout
about five inches long were all that rewarded our
search.   We crossed and re-crossed this stream
twenty-two times in about seven miles, and
encamped on a sandy bottom covered with fine
pines.   Here I saw Steller's jays and Clement shot
one for me; I also saw a fox squirrel, but I could
not get it, and do not know its species.   A magnificent hawk flew over us; he had two white bands
on his tail — could it be *Falco lagopus?*

Fourth of July. Paso Chapadaro. Calm, misty,
silent.   The sun soon threw its red light over all
we saw to the west, but was hidden by the range of
mountains to the east which we had passed, till
mastering at an effort, as it seemed, the highest
ridge, it burst forth in all its splendor.   In the
bottom of my saddle-bags, rolled in a handker-
chief, was a flag given me by poor Hamilton
Boden, and by the time the haze had gone, it
floated in the breeze, from the top of the highest
tree near our camp; nature was all in a smile, and
we prepared to spend the day according to our
various inclinations.   Some slept, some basked in
indolence, some started off to look for game, some

looked to their saddle-bags and blankets; all was rest, at least from travel, and I unpacked my paper and pencils and made a sketch of the "Fourth of July Camp."

Wild cattle were abundant, and noon saw our camp in possession of a fine heifer shot by Rhoades. Steaks were broiled and fried, ribs roasted, brains stewed in the skull; delicacies under such circumstances unequalled by the cuisine of a palace.

When evening came, Mess No. 4, all good singers, gave us some beautiful choruses from operas, as well as simpler songs, and as night brought the solemn quiet, and the moon glided in its ordained course, "Old Hundred" was sung with the most solemn feelings of reverence and adoration.

July 5th. Gabilana. Four o'clock saw us on our way. We rode some hours along the valley, rich in grass, shade-trees and springs of delicious water; then came a steep ascent, and most of us had to walk. We lost another mule today, but before leaving it succeeded in getting it to the table-land at the top of the gorge we had just ascended. It was a beautiful grove of pines and plenty of short green grass was under foot, and, most welcome sight, a log house looking so like home that a dozen of the boys rode off to see "a white woman;" but their disappointment was great — it was simply the house of a Mexican who had been in Texas some years, and had learned how to live in a little comfort.

July 6th. Santa Borgia. The woods today were most luxuriant as we wound round the gorge that commenced again our ascent to some still higher mountains. Our common robin was abundant, and a large green parrot, with a red head, was seen in every clump of pines, but its uncouth squalling was distracting. Except the cardinal and other gros-beaks how few birds of splendid plumage have sweet voices.

July 7th. Pitochi. Today we have followed one of the most extraordinary gorges we have seen, crossing and winding along the banks of a beautiful little stream, till between giant precipices we had almost the sensation that they might tumble in to fill the gap and crush us. One particularly fine white cliff, we judged nine hundred feet above us; topped off with high towers of nearly white sandstone, its sharp lines broken by a straggling pine or scraggy cedar, growing in some of the many fissures, it was so grand that we left it with regret.

July 9th. Cerro Prieto. I saw today the first water-ousel I ever saw alive in America, and was enchanted with his movements, as he jerked his wren-shaped body with sprightly activity, or with whirring flight went from stone to stone, or suddenly plunged, in the most unnatural manner, into the foaming little torrent, and spread his wings half open, the pinions lowest. He headed up stream, keeping at the bottom, and went about feeding in the crevices of the rocks with as much ease, if not as rapidly, as a bird in the air.

July 10th. Early as we start, no one murmurs. I am writing a few yards apart from Mess No. 12, a queer lot. Rhoades, who has crossed the plains from Fort Independence to Santa Fé eleven times, and Barrat, a wagoner of the Mexican War, are both very original, and perhaps would not get on well with the others but for Dr. Trask, a truly good man, who is their Captain. It is a misty morning, fire more of smoke than warmth, tent wet, blankets cold and clammy, and we are waiting for them to dry before packing. The roll has been called, and each mess is preparing breakfast. I hear Dr. Trask courteously ask: "Are those plates clean?" and Rhoades's nonchalant answer: "To be sure they are, didn't we eat off 'em last night."

July 12th. Concepcion. Yesterday we passed oaks with a heavy leaf, glazed on the top, so as to look as rich as the magnolia grandiflora of Louisiana. Raspberries are abundant but not ripe, and strawberries plentiful. We camped on ground covered with dwarf huckleberries, and a species of plantain of which our mules ate freely, but the horses sparsely.

July 14th. We commenced our day with the ascent of a steep rocky hill, with the trail cut in by the mules much in the manner of those we had seen before, and the road at first was so steep that we had to lead our horses. One of our mules gave out completely and we had to leave it on the table land which is almost invariably the apex of these mountains. A beautiful grove of pines with short but good grass beneath, made a fine contrast of color. As we camped our usual storm came on more violent than usual, and we were drenched through. Lieut. Browning says: "The claps of thunder and flashes of lightning are very well done in this country."

July 18th. Our road today was by far the most tedious we have had, being up hill nearly all the time, but the view from the top almost repaid us, if not our mules, for the toil. We arrived at the highest top near Jesus Maria; miles of mountain tops and peaks of rock and woods are far below us. Through a gap we looked at clouds blending with the mists below them, until the scene was like an ocean view.

Four hours and a half of most precipitous descent brought us to a luxuriant growth of pine and spruce, and passing through one of the wildest and most picturesque gorges I have ever seen, we came to the extraordinary little town of Jesus Maria, situated at the junction of two little torrents of clear, beautiful water, tumbling in noisy, joyous splashing from rock to basin, and carrying away the rubbish from this half-civilized settlement of miners as it passes through the town.

July 19th. Jesus Maria. Gold and silver are both found here, and the rock which contains these ores is soft and easily ground; the most common way of grinding seems to be a flutter wheel fastened to a shaft, which turns on another within the inner circle; this inner one is water tight, and two large stones are pulled round by ropes of rawhide fast to the wheel, which is about three feet from the ground. These are trailed round and smash the ore for two or three days; it is then dried, pulverized and washed. Sometimes simple washing, and sometimes with amalgam of quicksilver, gives the result of eight to ten marks of silver to the cargo, viz: — three hundred pounds. Gold is much more variable in its profits.

Everything used here is brought from the Pacific side, quicksilver, irons, wines and liquors; even flour is sometimes brought, but most of that comes from Sonora which is ten days' travel to the east.

July 20th. There was no open space large enough for us to picket our mules and pitch our tents in this town (said to contain two thousand inhabitants) and eventually we had to hire the only corral in the place, full of fleas and dirt, for which we had to pay twelve dollars per day. It is only about seventy yards long and perhaps thirty broad, so that we are very crowded. We find here three Americans, two Swiss and one Italian, who have for many years resided in this country as traders. There were a number of Englishmen, owners and superintendents of mines, who all treated us most kindly. I think the view of Jesus Maria which I give, supersedes the necessity of a verbal description of its situation, but not of the town itself, which is the place of all others that would be selected by a man who had left behind him enemies sworn to vengeance, for two minutes' start up any of the mountains would insure a safe retreat.

Yet the place has its charms; superb rocks, wild passes, and withal a vegetation so luxuriant that with the dozens of birds I could have spent weeks of enjoyment, but we leave tomorrow as we have been here two days.

July 22d. Leaving the public square yesterday we took a winding alley up the precipitous mountain: two of our mules fell off the trail; one rolled over ten or twelve times, pack and all, and then to our utter amazement got up, having come by a series of falls to a small level space, and began to eat.

We spent four hours going six miles to where the rear of the company encamped; thirty mules

JESUS MARIA, LOOKING NORTHWEST

July 20, 1849

and thirteen men went six miles further, and Mr. Browning found himself with three men, four miles ahead of all, with no other assistance, and eighteen mules to care for. These distances between us are the result of the unequal strength of our mules, and one mule and a horse left behind us. A drizzling rain came up as night fell, and we had a miserable night.

July 23d. Limestone, sandstone, and huge masses of amalgam of gravel and sand, with quartz, have been all about us. The small plants are numerous; ferns everywhere, a beautiful scarlet honeysuckle is very plentiful, spruce, pine, balsam fir, hemlock and pitch-pine are all seen; our swamp alder grows here to great size, looking like black beech. Raspberries are as good as in Maine, and very abundant in many of the ravines and valleys. The magnificent oak with glossy leaves is here too, and a new species of reed, a perfect miniature of our large cane of the west. Steller's jay, a titmouse, and, I think, a crossbill, have been seen, but no parrots such as we saw to the east of Jesus Maria. Mists and fogs hang over the mountains, and the air is cold and damp unless the sun shines, and then it is very hot. Deep, indeed, is the solitude of this grand country, for but little animation is seen. Often as I sit sketching or writing I hear only the chirp of some cricket, or distant scream of a hawk to tell me that living things are about me.

July 25th. We have been feasting on venison, here very plentiful, and much sought after by the men, to such an extent indeed that Nicholas Walsh having wounded a deer yesterday, which was both misty and cloudy, followed it over hill and dale and lost himself.

We made a large fire hoping he might see it, fired guns and shouted, and early today he was found by a Mexican scout; he had wandered about for thirty hours between leaving the party and returning to it. He had been greatly frightened, and looked wild, when the Mexican brought him in. He said he kept getting almost within range of the wounded animal when it disappeared, and heavy rain began falling which washed out the blood of the trail which would have showed him the way back. He thought his heart would burst when he realized he was lost in an Indian country; he had no idea where he was; everything was mist and greyness; he was cold, hungry, and soaked through, and worst of all his gun and ammunition were wet; he was so eager not to lose sight of the deer that he had forgotten the rule always to reload as soon as a charge is fired, when in an enemy's country, as the report of the gun will inform the Indian of your proximity. He never heard one of the guns that were fired every fifteen minutes from our camp, and as soon as dawn came searching parties started in every direction, little knowing that Walsh was trotting towards us, behind a Mexican, in the peculiar half run of that grade of native, when in haste.

David Hudson and I had struck far off to the north, and had traversed table lands and mountain paths for some miles, when just as we emerged from a patch of oaks and undergrowth, all dead, thin, dried, brown leaves in contrast with the full summer bloom of everything outside this blighted spot, we heard the tread of men, and quietly moving behind two large trees near us, waited to see who the newcomers were. We knew we had heard the footsteps of more than one man, but only the Mexican appeared at first; in a few seconds with eyes like owls in daylight, mouth open, hair streaming in every direction, and looking like an escaped Bedlamite, came Walsh. He gripped my hand so that it feels bruised yet; his first words were: "Good fellow if he is a Greaser, have you two dollars?" The Mexican told us he had left the mine where he worked, to go to the rancho where his sweetheart lived, and knowing the country well, took a cross trail for speed and heard a man making a great noise who seemed to want something; he soon found him and knew at once he belonged to our company whom he had seen at Jesus Maria.

July 27th. We parted today with Joseph Stevenson, one of our blacksmiths, to my great regret. He returned to Jesus Maria where he is going into partnership with a Mr. Williams, a carpenter, and will no doubt make a good living for he is a very excellent workman. I passed today a large pine tree with the most 'curious display of the sagacity, instinct, or whatever it may be called, of some insectivorous bird, I think a red-headed woodpecker; for I saw one a few minutes afterwards, and he may be the workman. The bark of the tree was perforated with holes just large enough in diameter to hold the small acorn of this country, say half an inch, and about as deep; the holes were from a quarter of an inch to an inch and a half apart; the acorns seemed all to be put in butt end foremost, I suppose because the cone end would turn the rain better. Should instinct tell all this to the beautiful bird who lays up his store in this manner so that he may go in the winter to eat the grub that is sure to be in every acorn, how wonderful are the provisions of Nature for her children.

This high ridge gives a complete change of birds; Steller's jay, so common a few days' journey from here, is rare — indeed, I have only seen one; the Ultramarine takes its place, and I hope in a few days to see the Columbian; a few ravens are to be seen, and one hawk, like our red-tailed, but

I am not sure of him. The lightning here is most vivid, and on the sides of some of the mountains of medium height, I found seared and scathed patches of timber and undergrowth, as if ignition of the electric fluid had taken place at those spots, possibly attracted to them by the presence of iron; if this is so, how terrific would be the destruction to our company if such an event occurred where we were encamped.

July 28th. Paragarto. We did not leave camp until nearly noon, waiting for a train of one hundred and eighty-two mules packed with nothing but flasks of quicksilver; the usual length of trains is about forty to fifty, with six or eight men. Our road was the usual ascent and descent, and on the second descent I saw fifteen or twenty swifts, about double the size of our common chimney swift at home. They appeared to nest on the cliffs opposite to the trail, a location similar to that of the first Republican swallow my father[1] found near Cincinnati.

Sundown found us in a beautiful little valley, setting up our tents in the usual rain, and trying to

---

[1] The Cliff Swallow (*Petrochelidon lunifrons*) is described in Audubon's *Birds of America*, ed. 1840, vol. i, p. 177. Audubon proposed the name *Hirundo republicana* in 1824, but Say had named the species *Hirundo lunifrons* the year before. I am indebted to Dr. F. H. Snow for reference to the synonymy and the account of the discovery of this species in Coues's *Birds of the Colorado Valley*, part i, pp. 426-429.

dry ourselves by the fires of those who had
come in ahead. We have now become so accustomed to daily rains that it is a matter of course
to encounter them. There is a rancho here with
peaches and figs in abundance. In this valley we
went again to shoeing horses; never were shoes
lost in so short a time as on these cruel trails, sometimes they are wrenched off in a few hours, and
they commonly get loose and require nails every
three or four days. Layton and I ascended one
of the highest peaks in the neighborhood; like all
other mountain regions when one peak, seemingly
the highest, is reached, others still higher appear
between us and the desired view. Out of breath,
shoes cut, and clothes torn, we reached the foot of
the highest elevation like the cone of Vesuvius,
and found it an arduous climb; broken, reddish
traprock of all sizes made the mass, and a straggling pine from time to time added to the solemnity
of this desolate place, which filled me with awe
and reverence, which was not decreased as mut-
tering thunder gave us warning that our turn
would be next, if the attractions of the mountains
the storm was already besieging, did not exhaust
the clouds. Silently, however, we struggled up-
wards, and another half hour enabled us to look
to the east, south, and west as far as eye could
reach; the north was left to our imaginations,
being hid by a veil of clouds which sent flash after

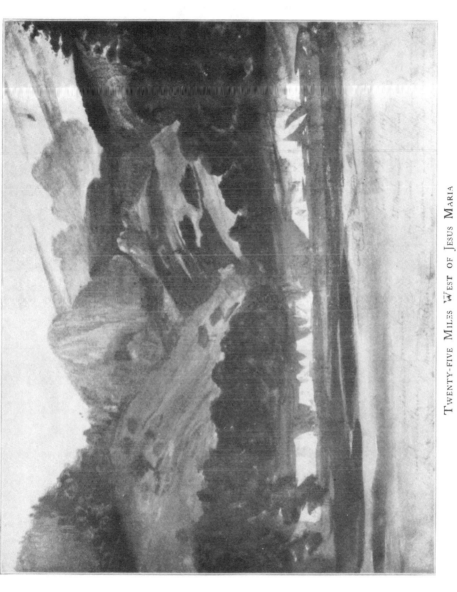

Twenty-five Miles West of Jesus Maria

July 25, 1849

flash, peal after peal, to tell us of the storm which held sway there. Distance lent such enchantment to all that the valleys and slopes looked as velvety as an English lawn.

Our descent was very rapid, but giving the usual fatigue of a downhill march. I saw many runs of deer, no doubt made by the bucks following the doe, though they are still in velvet. I saw some squirrels but could not get at them, as the stones on which we were walking were so loose that they would sometimes roll two hundred feet (I might almost say yards), and made so much noise that they startled not only them, but the deer.

At the bottom of the hill we both bathed in the little torrent that waters the beautiful valley; at times it is two or three hundred yards wide, and again compressed so much as only just to leave room to let the stream through. Its chilly bracing foam sent a sparkle through us as if bathing in soda water, and we may boast of having had such a bath as few can enjoy, unsurpassed for its freshness, and in the very heart of the southern Rocky mountains, perhaps a spot never seen by any other white men.

August 6th, Trinidad. The loss of mules, a few terrific passes, and here and there a valley of extreme beauty brought us to the western ridge of the chain of mountains leading down to Trinidad, a little old, worn-out place, having only some few hundred inhabitants, the town itself containing some stores like those we have come across everywhere from Davis's Rancho to Jesus Maria. At Trinidad there are three Frenchmen, one the Alcalde, the other two traders, dealing in everything from horses to a single tallow candle. They also sell quantities of muscalle, which is taken mainly for the love of the alcohol, for any dose of medicine would be as palatable, and in this hot country probably more beneficial, certainly less injurious. I asked one of the Frenchmen, now so long a resident that he had almost forgotten his own language, what induced him to live in such a country. His answer was short and to the point: "The love of gold." "Have you found it?" I asked. "No," was his reply, "but I cannot return without it." So it is with many of all nations, who, lured by the stories of fortunes easily made, come to this part of the earth and grow more and more lazy and indolent, until they have become unfit for the active, energetic industry requisite in happier and more enlightened portions of the world. The people here simply vegetate; many of them drink, and are depraved in many ways. Some seem happy with their Mexican wives, who, however, are neither as handsome nor as clever as quadroons.

Nature is beautiful at every turn, now in bird and beast, then in tree and flower, then in rock and rill: how pained I am to pass them all by; but the position into which I have been forced demands every hour, and I am never my own master.

August 8th. Santa Rosa. Today I passed three partridges and two doves, warblers and flycatchers without number, all new, and many most beautiful. Santa Rosa where we are camped is a beautifully situated little village, with a silver mine as its chief interest. There are some fine horses here, possessing more of the Arabian look than any I have seen before in Mexico. With great regret, I exchanged my old favorite Monterey for a mare here worth six or eight dollars. With all my care of Monterey, I could not save his back, and I felt as if parting with a friend, when with his majestic stride, his ears set forward, giving to his small head and curved neck an expression of excitement and fierceness peculiarly his own, he almost sailed through our camp, and winding down a pass leading to the village, left me gazing at the spot where I had seen him last. There is fine grass and plenty of water, and I was told he had gone to a kind master, an Englishman who had drifted out here.

August 10th. We left our camp after great difficulty in getting our mules together, and at six camped again, fifteen miles only, on our way, for it has been up and down hill all the time. The sunny side of the hills is always very hot to us, and trying to our poor mules. We passed many changes of vegetation but musquit is still the prominent portion. One tree we saw had a large fruit five or six inches long, hanging like a pear; it contained seed, laid in like those of the milk-weed, and we were told the cotton-like substance which enclosed the seeds was used for candlewick. Here we saw the first large cacti I had seen of the cylindrical form; some of them are apparently forty feet high. If in a shaded situation, they have only one or two shoots, while others in open ground have perhaps fifty, but smaller and less luxuriant, being only six or eight inches in diameter, instead of four or more.

August 11th. Coming down the creek our second day's descent we opened into a wide arroyo of sometimes two hundred yards, with water running through it, and again the water disappeared and the dry parched bottom sent up a heat such as I do not recollect having ever felt before. I saw the men fag, get down and tumble on the grass at the sides, whenever a shady spot could be found, and the poor mules seemed completely exhausted. Many of us became sick at our stomachs from the effects of the intense contrast in temperature, for we had left an atmosphere like that of Maine, for the tropics. We saw a storm coming up and for once wished it to hasten; but we had no rain, only a gust of its cooling breeze, and we gladly left our trying surroundings for a delightful shade and green grass.

August 14th. We have had the same sort of
travelling today; we came to the Yaqui River, a
muddy stream at this season, about two hundred
yards wide and so deep that we had to employ
canoes to carry over our cargoes; the canoes are
paddled by Mexicans (no great boatmen, by the
way); the mules and horses we swam over, having
passed Tomochi [Tonichi]; the little town is said
to be four days' travel from Ures; it is about three
quarters of a mile from the river, and it is a
deserted mining place of a few adobe houses.
Here, as usual, was sold muscalle, a few fieholes
[frejoles][1] and wheaten tortillas. Only once have
I seen pulque, at a small distillery of muscalle.

August 15th. Soyopa. Leaving the Rio Yaqui
for its little tributaries, which are sometimes above
ground, and sometimes below, running over the
sands, or disappearing underneath them, we
encamped in a quiet cool spot, to rest after the
great heat of the sunny sides of the hills we had
left and the arroyos made by mountain torrents
where we were nearly suffocated, and we look
forward to the plains of the Gulf of California and
the sea breeze that sweeps them, with anticipations
of delight. Alas! an occasional thunderstorm is all
that gives coolness to the atmosphere here, for the
puffs of land breeze only tantalize and do not cool.

I tried here to buy or trade horses, and regret I

---

[1] *Frejoles* or *frijoles*, Spanish for beans.

did not get one I saw, but the straightened circumstances of the company compelled me to give up the idea.

August 17th.   We passed a large rancho of about a hundred and fifty men and their squaws, for nearly all were Indians, and camped six miles further on; but as night came on thieves came too, whether Mexicans or Apaches I know not, but we have never encountered bolder ones.   Hinckley, Havens, Sloat, Valentine and Boggs were on guard, all good men, but of no avail, four double barrelled guns and two pistols were taken, one from under Boggs' very eyes — how, no one could tell.   We looked for the trail and found it, large feet and small moccasins and barefooted; but the dew was unswept from the grass outside the camp, so the theft must have been earlier in the night: we could recover nothing, though four of our best men went back; so after a fruitless search of some hours we left for Ures, and at three o'clock entered into a series of hills and valleys so beautiful in form and color, so fresh and green that our spring could not equal them.   Many of Cole's[1] pictures were brought to mind.

---

[1] Thomas Cole (1801-1848), an American landscape painter of English birth, was one of the earliest artists to depict the beauties of American scenery; he was noted for his scenes in the Catskills.   His recent death doubtless emphasized his pictures in Audubon's mind.

August 22d. Ures. Three days' travel over a prairie sometimes covered with chaparral, and sometimes with grass brought us here. We are greatly disappointed; Ures, the capital of Sonora, with its Governor and military, Alcalde and court, is an adobe village of about four thousand Indians, and still they have power, and the Alcalde proved himself a man of considerable ability.

Coming down the mountains to the Rio Yaqui, we left coolness for heat. First we saw Turkey Buzzards, and lower down the Carrion Crow; still farther down we came to the table prairies and there were the Carra Carra Eagles[1] in great numbers; sometimes we saw fifty in a day, so that birds mark the altitude. The mocking-bird, raven and jay of the mountains are with us no more. I have found the plumed partridge plentiful, one with a black breast and guinea-fowl spots; but they are less numerous here and I fear will soon be seen no more. We are told gold abounds in the surrounding mountains, but the Apaches are so bad that it cannot be secured; however, the exaggerations of these people are so amazing, that we do not believe their tales; if we did it would be useless to leave

---

[1] The Caracara or Brazilian Eagle is described in Audubon's *Birds of America,* ed. 1840, vol. i, p. 21. It was found in Florida by Audubon but so rarely occurs in the United States that it is not included in the "A. O. U. Check List of North American Birds." The name is derived from the hoarse cry that it utters.

here, as we could never live to reach our destination, there are so many difficulties; one great one is always with us, that is our poor mules, which fail daily.

August 28th. Some gentlemen today presented me with a large glass jar of peaches, beautifully preserved; there must have been at least a gallon, and we were so very grateful, for we become very weary of our monotonous fare of coarse bread made from unbolted flour, beef or game, half cooked often, and eaten from tin plates or the frying pan, and tin cups for coffee, *if* we have it.

We heard here one piano, but the same peculiar nasal twang pervades the singing of the whole of Northern Mexico.

On the journey here we lost eight mules and horses, and but for Clement I should have been hard pressed for the latter for Barratt. Clement exchanged his horse for two Mexican ones, which he procured from Mr. Gabilondo. The very next day I heard Clement's horse was dead, so I went at once to see Mr. Gabilondo. He said he had sold the horse and a bargain was a bargain, and that probably the animal had eaten something poisonous; however, revenge was talked of by all the men, and I found a fine looking mule in our train very mysteriously. To my question as to where the mule came from, I was told he had been "traded for;" I told the man who was riding him that he would have to bear all risks, and he cheerfully said he would; and so he did, for when the owner came forward, with his brand in hand — the voucher, in this country, of ownership — he was told very politely that the trade had been made for a pair of pistols (a pair that had been stolen four days previously), and he could not return the mule unless the pistols were forthcoming. There was a good deal of "Carambo,"[1] etc., but the train moved on through half the rabble of Ures, some of whom laughed, some swore.

August 30th. Leaving Ures the country is more level; to the southeast is a large plain covered with musquit of a different species from that on the eastern side, and not quite so thorny; the large cactus of the mountains is not found here, two smaller species taking its place.

I did not leave Ures until five p. m., when the train was five or six miles ahead of me. I rode slowly along the swampy lane leading north from the town, bordered with heavy hedges of reeds and chaparral, with, from time to time, a cactus, a palm, or a cabbage tree breaking the line of the horizon. One tall palm, stiff and formal, was standing out very distinctly in the soft light between moonrise and sunset. Large flocks of the yellow troupial in noisy bustle settling themselves in the rushes and willows bordering the little

---

[1] *Caramba* is the commonest of Spanish interjections.

stream we are now fording, brought to my mind many an evening return home.

Two or three miles of this travelling brought me to the first sandy tableland, and the dull monotony of a road shut in by chaparral continued until I came to the camp, low-spirited and tired, and longing for the end of this toilsome journey; perhaps the fact that Osgood, Plumb and Brown having left us at Ures to go by way of Mazatlan with another company, may have had more to do with my depression than other circumstances.

Here, in the heart of the Indian country, with the watchword "Apache," in the mouth of every Mexican, and our guard rigid, we are toiling on through an interesting country. The large cactus, given by Fremont or Abert,[1] we met here in great luxuriance, having a centre of pulpy pith surrounded by a number of long hearts, one for each ridge of the meat, or pulp, of the plant. If I only had time, how I should enjoy making drawings of all this, but I cannot.

---

[1] Many scientific reports appeared in the public documents of this period. Fremont's "Report of an Expedition to Oregon and California" was printed both in Senate and House documents and in a separate edition in 1845. The Senate documents of the 1st session of the 30th Congress, printed in 1848, contain Emory's "Reconnoissance from Fort Leavenworth to San Diego," Abert's "Examination of New Mexico," Wislizenus's "Memoir of a Tour to Northern Mexico," and Fremont's "Geographical Memoir upon Upper California." Audubon probably had in mind the cylindrical cactus figured by Abert.

September 2d. Two days out from Ures we came to some Pimos Indians washing gold from black was, which they said produced well; we found some lumps of ore in the dust, all of irregular shapes. The value is only about one real (about ten cents) for each bushel of dirt. Each man made about two dollars a day.

We had fine grass and pond water here, and are off for Altar.

September 9th. Altar. We reached this place yesterday after eight days journey over barren, sandy hills exactly like these which surround this town. What an eight days it has been, I hate to recall to my mind even by writing these brief notes. Half of us are on foot, our clothes are ragged and torn, and we have lived on half rations, often less, of beans, and what we *call* bread. Several days we were twenty and twenty-four hours without water, no grass for our horses, and inexpressibly weary *always*. Yet we are well and not as much depressed as might be supposed, and while we are short of nearly everything, money included, our courage is in no degree lessened.

Altar is a miserable collection of adobe houses, with perhaps a thousand inhabitants; there are only one or two grandees here, but nearly all are of Indian mixture. At one of the little villages through which we passed, La Nada, we had all the town about us, admiring our white (?) faces, and asking hundreds of questions, many of the girls had pretty Indian faces, and beautiful teeth and hair. Great quantities of peaches grow in the valleys and irrigated gardens, but what comfort there is is very primitive. Plenty of the California partridge are here, but the black-breasted is nowhere to be seen; the California quail is found, and Gamble's blue partridge.

I saw yesterday the most wonderful rainbow, or rather mass of prismatic mist; a heavy thunderstorm, one of the most furious we have encountered, took us just as we had left a rancho, formerly an old Mission, with a very fine reservoir two hundred yards square, built of stone and the exhaust arch of brick, and we rode on in drenching rain for nearly an hour. The storm abated just before sunset, leaving all of the west, below the lifting clouds, of that indescribable, furious red, which follows such blows, and the receding storm receiving the light and blending into an immense mass of rainbow haze.

The people here are not at all friendly to us, and instead of having them come out to see us at our camp, as at other places, often in such numbers as to be a nuisance, we find them cold, and almost uncivil. We are not looked upon with the same interest as heretofore, and could neither buy nor beg what we required for our use. We, however, succeeded with some difficulty in getting good flour and pinole, at eight and ten dollars per cargo. We had to make a kiln and burn the wood for charcoal, which we needed to make horse-shoes, and we paid sixty-two and a half cents a pound for the only bar of iron we could find.

CHAPTER V

September 14th. Leaving Altar on the 10th we crossed a desert-like plain or prairie for many miles to the Rancho "La Sone," as usual a miserable cluster of mud jacals and surly Mexican vacheros, but we did not care for that. We bought and killed one of their cattle, paying four dollars for it; the next day the seller returned and asked seven, which we refused.

On the lagoon near here we found the American Avoset, long-billed curlew, and Canada crane; I thought I saw the sandhill, but it was so far off I could not be certain; the red-shafted woodpecker is seen daily, and many small birds, new to me, but not so abundant as two hundred miles behind us. The soil of this country is beautiful in many places, but the want of water and timber renders it difficult to live here; the government is feeble, and desolation and poverty show that better days have been seen. Tomorrow we start westward at 4 a. m. for our march to the Colorado; how we shall get through the twenty leagues with almost no water or grass I do not know, but it must be done.

Some of the men hearing the rattle of the snake of that name, in a small bunch of musquit and

cactus, took shovels to dig him out, and after clear-
ing away the brush soon found the holes the snakes
live in. At about two feet down they came to a
tolerably large female, which had in her nest nine
young; beautiful little creatures, about a foot long;
they had great courage, and coiled and struck with
fury at anything placed near them.

September 17th. Near Papagos[1] villages. Last
night, as for many preceding evenings, we sat down
to our supper of bread and water, our sugar, coffee
and all other matters culinary having been used
up, and the country affords no game. We all
felt the want of coffee or meat, after being up from
5 a. m. to 7 p. m., but we shall I hope, soon be
through this desolate country. Four days since
one of the party killed the largest and finest buck
antelope I ever saw, and we expected a treat, but
it was like the meat of a poor two-year-old beef,
hardly so good. We found the horns of a Rocky
Mountain sheep, and of the black-tailed deer, but
none have been killed, or even seen as yet.

The little water-holes we came to, were filled
with animalculæ, and contained many turtles and
snakes, and a few frogs and toads. For lizards this
country cannot be surpassed; one little beauty with
a banded tail runs before us and across our path by

---

[1] The Papago Indians belonged to the Piman family, but
had separated from the Pimas at the time of their conversion
by the Spanish missionaries.

dozens. It makes frequent stops, and each time curls its tail on its back, and waves it gently four or five times most gracefully, finally retreating to some hole in the sand, or to a thicket of cactus which abounds.

We have met no Indians of the old Aztec race; fifty Papagos would count all we have seen, and they are fast passing away judging from the dilapidations of the towns, and the numbers of empty houses. The people live on turtles, and what game they can get. I have seen some elk and antelope skins dressed and terrapin shells are everywhere. We have bought two terrapin fresh killed, some roots, and the fruit of a plant like the maguey; we have seen one or two fine horses, small, but well formed, ridden with only a rope around the neck; others had saddles; all the men ride lightly and well.

We came to some of their burial mounds, and saw the kettles and culinary articles of this poor people left for the dead, to aid them on their journey to the happy hunting grounds prepared for them by the Great Spirit. They are happy in their faith, and with no dissenting voices about this method of salvation or that.

At one place just after leaving the second rancho of Papago Indians on September 18th, we crossed what might certainly be called a part of the desert. Strips of red gravel a mile or two long, and two or three hundred yards wide, were frequently crossed, and other strips looking like dried parched-up white clay; the mountains are very irregularly formed, and of a blackish stone, looking in the distance almost purple. I tried to take some sketches, but could not make time.

On September 19th I procured two specimens of the *Dipodomys Phillippsii*;[1] the red tail and marsh hawks are abundant, and ravens are seen, as well as buzzards from time to time. We find many mounds of the *Dipodomys Phillippsii*, and prairie dog or some other marmot, but they are so shy that we have not killed one yet. We picked up yesterday horns of the Rocky Mountain sheep, and the Papagos tell us they are found in plenty in the mountains around us.

September 21st. The last village we passed of these Indians was situated on a large prairie of miserably poor soil, sandy and dry, covered with a peculiar small-leaved plant, containing a great deal of astringent, gummy sap; we find this only on the poorest of soils full of gravel and sand, and always hail it with dislike, though its taste, a little of it, is pleasant, being slightly aromatic, and yet in some way reminding one of baked apple. Why it is that these Indians settle in such country, I

---

[1] The *Dipodomys Phillippsii* is a species of mouse provided with a pouch and is popularly called the pocket or kangaroo mouse.

cannot conceive, for even the lizards, in most places innumerable, are scarce here. The Indians kill them with a light wand, giving them a dexterous tap on the head; they pick up the game (?), slip the head under a belt or string round their waists, and when sufficient are collected a little fire is made, and this delicate repast is enjoyed by them, as an epicure would relish his brace of woodcock.

I am told that a sort of mush is made of grasshoppers which abound all over the country, some of which are very beautiful; the insects are caught and dried, then pounded, and mixed with what meal or "pinole" they have; the "pinole" generally consists of parched wheat or corn, spiced and pounded, or ground dry on the "metale," the stone used by the Mexicans for making the meal used for their tortillas; the dish is considered quite a delicacy by both the Indians and Mexicans; the man who told me this said he had tasted it, found it pleasant, and except for the idea, a pretty good dish.

The horses of the Indians here are very tolerable but they are spoiled by being ridden too young. They use them steadily when two years old, and I saw even colts with the hair of the tail still curly, under boys fourteen or fifteen years of age.

The houses are cones, four or five feet high and eight to fifteen feet across, thatched in the rudest manner; in front of nearly every one however, there is a shade, made by planting four poles, and erecting on them a platform, first of sticks and brush, and finally earth on which some plants and grasses grow. I saw one covered with a gourd vine falling in festoons and strings, and bearing its hard fruit in profusion; the pleasant verdure looked very inviting as we rode by in the broiling sun. Two or three squaws were sitting under it, on the palmetto mats, coarsely made, occupying themselves with their daily avocations, some sewing on thin cotton stuff, some preparing the food. The women were generally large and square-faced, with low foreheads and ugly mouths, but fine eyes; they are generally dark, and very occasionally a fairly good-looking girl is seen. We took an Indian guide here, and offered him first a dollar a day; he took the money and held out his hands for more; two men were with him, one of whom asked what else would we give; he was shown a half-worn shirt; again he asked for more, a white shirt was given him, he looked at the shirts and the money, and pointed to a bright butcher knife; it was given to him. He gave a smile of satisfaction, jumped on his horse, which stood ready beside him, pointed out the road, motioned ahead and galloped off to his own house, some quarter of a mile distant. Two or three of our party followed him, myself among the number, and saw him lay his treasures down before his father and family; he then put on the worn red shirt, and with a low bow to all round him followed our company.

After a long and tedious ride over a gravelly prairie, with many cacti, musquit and wild sage growing on it, we passed between two ironstone mountains, up a valley to a well of sulphur water which was also pretty well impregnated with salt, where all took a drink, and going over the next ridge camped in poor grass and took our animals back to water them at the well.   Some of the mules drank five buckets of water, one after the other (the common shaker buckets) and the average amount each animal drank may be put down at three and a half.   The want of water is the greatest privation you can give a mule, as the flesh literally seems to dry off them, and without water a mule will rapidly fall off from being a good-looking animal, to a skeleton; but good grass and water, not too salt, will in a week restore them wonderfully.

On our march today we came to a dry run, what Pennypacker calls "a thunder-shower river," and after digging four feet found better water than we had had for some time.   We were all thirsty and drank of it freely.   I took two long draughts, and in half an hour was ready for more, and the poor mules had to be kept away by a guard.   Some of these "thunder-storm rivers" rise so rapidly as to surround camps in less time than it takes to remove the provisions and other property, and I was told by some of the parties we met near the Gila, that on the El Paso route a party of General Worth's train lost their baggage by just such floods as we have to look out for.

Leaving this water-hole Boggs and myself walked to the peaks of one of the conical mountains of iron-stone, which here surround the plains; it was bluish-black with heavy dashes of purple intermingled for yards at a time, and looked like huge masses of earth that had been frozen, and were just in the crumbling state which precedes thawing. The view from the top was very grand, but all the scenes we had as we ascended from the plain gave pleasure. At first the broad prairie stretched west as far as the line of horizon; a few feet higher on the mountain enabled us to see the conical heads of others, and as we went higher and higher, we saw hill after hill, and mountain capped mountain, and the straight line which formed our horizon at first was lost in the irregular one of peaks of the wildest character and desolation. As we looked north round the entire country to north again, our eyes surveyed miles of apparently waste barren country, without wood, water or animated nature; one vulture alone sailed magnificently round us, surveying us from a closer circle at every whirl he made, his wings rustling as they glided past only a few feet from us. We admired his grace and envied his power, as we watched the sun go down, and fancied that just beyond the hills we saw were the waves of the Gulf of California. We descended to camp in the evening shadows and made our meal of bread and water with good appetites.

September 22d. I remained behind this morning with one of the men to hunt up some missing mules, so that the main party were some ten miles on the road ahead, but we overtook them at nine that night, and camped down without water or grass.

September 23d. Daylight saw us on the march again, and at twelve we found good grass, and halted for four hours, leaving at sundown for the Gila, expecting to reach it by daylight, but our mules were so hungry we could not drive them, and we encamped again without grass or water.

September 24th. At daylight again we were off, and one o'clock brought us to the long-looked-for Pimos Valley, with a rancho of one small house and a few broken-down mules. However, here we found water and a camp ground.

September 25th. Off again as soon as light with ourselves and animals somewhat refreshed by a long day's rest, plenty of corn, water and melons. Before our arrival here we had looked forward with pleasure to meeting others from home travelling our road, hoping to have news of comparatively late date, as this valley is a sort of rendezvous; but we have no more than we bring, we pass and re-pass companies daily, but since we find they have no news for us we go on with a single salutation.

As we came unexpectedly upon the wagon trail of the Gila route, an exclamation of joy came from almost every one, and tired as we were we journeyed until night in better spirits than we had been in for some time. The old chief of the Pimos came out to see us, and presented letters from Col. Cooke,[1] Col. Graham[2] and others, recommending him as honest, kind

---

[1] Philip St. George Cooke (1809-1895) served under Kearny in the conquest of New Mexico, was given command of the "Mormon battalion," which had been recruited at Council Bluffs from among the Nauvoo refugees, and was sent from Santa Fé to reinforce Kearny in California. The journal of the expedition was printed at the time (Senate ex. doc. No. 2, special session, 31st Cong.) and later in an expanded form as "The Conquest of New Mexico and California" (New York, 1878). Cooke commanded the federal troops during the territorial troubles in Kansas, served with distinction in the Civil War and was brevetted Major General at its close.

[2] James Duncan Graham was a member of Long's first expedition. In 1840 he was appointed commissioner for the survey of the Maine boundary and did good service in the settlement of that controversy. He was for a time principal astronomer of the Mexican Boundary Commission, but was recalled, on account of disagreements with Commissioner Bartlett, and made a separate report (Senate ex. doc. No. 121, 1st session, 32d Cong.). He reached the rank of colonel during the Civil War and died in 1865. Mt. Graham, Arizona, bears his name.

and solicitous for the welfare of Americans. I gave him three broken-down mules, and some other trifles for which he seemed grateful, but the extravagance of the Americans who have passed through has made it difficult for anyone to make reasonable bargains with either Pimos or Maricopas;[1] we had to give him a fiannel shirt for a little over a peck of corn, wheat or beans. Many who came to trade had already made up their minds only to do so for some particular article, and in those cases it was not of the least avail to offer anything else. Sometimes they would refuse a flannel shirt in exchange for a couple of melons, but by tearing the shirt into strips and sewing these together, two or three times the value of the garment may be obtained, as they are delighted with anything resembling a sash, or bands for the head. Jewelry had no value to them, fancy beads were worthless, stone beads however they traded for eagerly, but *we* had none. Red blankets and blue, red flannel torn into long strips they preferred to anything, though many of the women chose white shirts; like all squaws they are very good natured. They are dressed in a cotton, home-made sarape, if [wearing] a garment fastened round the waist, and leaving the whole upper part of the body

---

[1] The Pima Indians were called Pimos in the books of fifty years ago. The Maricopas belonged to the Yuman family but had united with the Pimas for protection.

exposed, can be called dressed; their hair is cut square across the forehead, and worn not very long.

We found some weed in the grass here very injurious to our horses and mules. I lost my mare here. Weed lost his, and nearly all ran down, so as to be scarcely fit for use. Having now four men without mounts, I was persuaded to buy a wagon and harness complete, as I could get one for twenty-five dollars.

The river bottom here forms a great flat, which was, I think, once irrigated; at all events, it is cut up by a great many lagoons, nearly all muddy, but the water is not so salt in those that do not run, as to be undrinkable; in some places the water is so impregnated that as the water evaporates, a cake of pure salt is deposited, and the Indians on being asked for it, brought us five or six pounds in a lump. It was pure white when broken, but on the surface a sediment covered it. The country is nearly flat, and on the light sandy soil there is found grass, in some places very sparse and thin, and in the others pretty good. No water but rain water, and that at long distances apart. We find on the few hills the columnar cactus in great abundance, a great many of the same class of plants as on the Rio Grande, and convolvuli without number; they seem to live on dew. The soil of the hills is rocky, and indeed, sometimes for miles, chalky limestone takes the place of rock entirely.

October 1st.   The first rise as we enter the desert gives the view of the plain for a great distance, and it seems one vast waste of twenty by a hundred miles.

The road is continuous clay and sand, so impregnated with salt and other mineral matter deleterious to vegetation, that sun flowers and salt grass, and the accursed emblem of barrenness and sterility "Larrea Mexicana," [Creosote plant] according to Dr. Trask, are all that are seen in the way of herbage.   In places the sunflowers are marvelously luxuriant, and cover miles of the country, and are from five to seven feet high, the road cut through them being the only gap in their almost solid ranks.

The dust in this road is over the shoe tops, and rises in clouds, filling eyes and almost choking us as we trudge along, sore and jaded — men, horses, mules, cattle.   We stop at night, after eight hours' travel, having made only fifteen or twenty miles; often without food except by chance, for our animals.   Grass is only found in the good bends of the river, which we may strike, or may not.

October 3d.   Left at eight in the morning, and rode fifteen miles, where we found water in some holes; we had noticed a very heavy rain yesterday in this direction, which had probably filled them. We rode on until night, when we camped until one in the morning, when, by the light of a full moon we re-packed and started on for the river which we reached at eight in the morning. Resting here for four hours, we started to make five miles or more; necessity demanded our doing this to arrive at good grass.

Passing along the sandy trail we saw hundreds of the plumed partridge (the brown-headed). I shot five in about ten minutes. I could not delay longer, as my fast-walking little mule was too jaded to put to the pain of going faster to catch up with the train. These birds, at this season, seem to feed on the seeds of the pig-weed, which is now and then seen in patches of many acres, putting one in mind of old potato fields. The sandy desolation of the river bottom is beyond belief; nothing but the sand hills of the Carolina coast can compare with it.

Oct. 5th. A few cotton-woods and scrub-willow, with dried weeds, and some sunflower plants, make thickets here and there, and this is all that is to be seen in the way of vegetation, for about a hundred miles below the Pimos villages, which hundred miles we made in five days, and are now, thanks to a placard at the forks of the road, across the far-famed Gila, in a grassy bottom of coarse swamp tufts, which is better than nothing, but our animals do not seem to like it much, though they eat it, in their starved condition.

The river here is a very rapid stream at this season, about a hundred and fifty yards wide, and from eighteen to twenty inches deep, with very deep holes in places. The bottom is shifting quicksand, delightfully varied with drift logs, put exactly where they can best trip up the mules; as the water is like that of the Mississippi, *below* St. Louis, you never see the logs until you are over them.

We look and long for Gila trout, and wild-fowl, but in vain. I shot two blue-wings and one of our men caught two little trout. Our road is garnished almost every league, with dead cattle, horses or oxen; and wagons, log chains, and many valuable things are left at almost every camping ground by the travellers; we ourselves have had to do the same, to relieve our worn and jaded mules, able now to carry only about a hundred pounds. Our personal effects amount to about one change each, with our ammunition and arms, all else discarded or used up or stolen.

Opposite our camp about three miles from us, is a hot spring of beautifully clear water; it is so hot as to just be bearable (we have now no thermometer) and is tasteless.

Night far on the prairie is always solemn, but when in a doubtful country, where one is uncertain as to the friendliness of the Indians, our watch became one of silence and caution. We saw a long line of regularly placed fires burn up, and, hour after hour, could see them flare up, as fresh fuel was placed on them. We had heard that Captain Thorn[1] with a hundred emigrants was just behind us, and we thought this might be his camp; but when morning came and a long line of dark objects met my eyes as I left my tent, I wondered if they could be mules, so regular in their distances and march. I soon saw it was a procession of a hundred and fifty squaws, each carrying the provisions like a pack mule for her husband, who, hero-like, armed with spear, shield and bow, proudly bore himself and his quiver, made of wild-cat, cougar, or other skin, full of arrows, on to the wars of the Maricopas and Apaches, *so it was said*; probably the object was to assist the Yumas against the Americans. Of this we had no proof, for all was quiet, owing no doubt to the good effect produced by the appearance of the Americans, and the prompt shooting of a party of Texans who had shot one or two Yumas Indians for not making the right landing. Such summary proceedings never occurred again. We also heard that Lieut. Coats [Couts][2] said that he had been the main cause of

[1] Herman Thorn, soldier in the Mexican War, distinguished himself in the battles of Churubusco and Molino del Rey, and was made captain. He was drowned October 16, 1849, as stated later in the text.

[2] Cave Johnson Couts, a Tennessean and West Pointer, went to California in 1848 as first lieutenant of dragoons in Graham's battalion. He resigned his commission and married the pretty daughter of a prominent Spanish family in 1851, settled in California and acquired considerable property, and died in 1874.

the favorable change in the Indians towards the Americans, especially on the part of the Yumas. We saw many of this tribe riding their horses with ropes in the animals' mouths, pads for saddles, and ropes around the bodies in which they can slip their feet.

October 14th. Sixteen days of travel from the Pimos village and *such travel*, as please God, I trust we may none of us ever see again, brought us to within three miles of the Gila.[1] If we thought ourselves badly off at Altar, we are much more reduced in every way than we were there. The food poor, monotonous and inefficient has been *forced* down, simply to sustain life. We have lost more mules, of course; our wagon delayed us at least ten miles a day, and we left it after using it three days. We were on the "qui vive" for Indians all the time. Lack of water and grass we have almost come to regard as inevitable; truly we looked, and are, a forlorn spectacle, and we feel, I am sure, worse than we look.

---

[1] Audubon returned to the Gila at the point of its junction with the Colorado. The usual emigrant road either kept to the south of the Gila or crossed the river at the bend and re-crossed it sometime before coming to the Colorado. Audubon must either have kept to the north of the river or omitted to mention the recrossing. The crossing of the Colorado was just below the mouth of the Gila. Lieut. Whipple was making observations at this point at this time. Fort Yuma was established here in 1852, opposite the present town of Yuma.

With all this there has been no useless com-
plaining, no murmuring, and with all our priva-
tions, greater than I care to enumerate, or even
to think about, we are none of us ill, though a good
many feel the effects of their hardships, and are
weakened by them. John Stevens walked *all* the
way from the last Pimos village, and declares he
never felt better; Henry Mallory, Bob Layton
and I have done almost as much walking and are
perfectly well.

All along the road we have been told we could
trade with the Yumas here, but a few pumpkins
seemed to be all they had at this season, and, as
our provisions were at the lowest ebb, we left for
the crossing of the Colorado.

We had the use of a boat in the crossing, which
belonged to a Mr. Harris who came from Texas,
near Houston. It was really a large wagon body,
made into a scow, and very useful we found it;
Mr. Harris treated us with the greatest kindness,
and aided us with provisions to the best of his
abilities, and we most sincerely wished him and
his amiable wife all happiness and comfort.

We found Lieut. Com. Coats most kind and
hospitable; with the aid of his sergeant's boat, a
wagon body caulked, we crossed with everything,
in two days. I found the Indians, who swam our
mules, the fastest and most powerful swimmers I
ever saw, being able to swim round the horses and

guide them with readiness and facility that aston-
ished us all; they swim over-handed. I could find
no one willing to sell or trade horses, and we are
about to start on this much-heard-of and much-
dreaded desert, having lost two mules which were
drowned after the company had crossed; they
returned to drink, and losing footing could not
regain it, and had not sufficient strength to battle
against the current.

Last evening I was invited to take supper with
Lieut. Coats, which I greatly enjoyed, for seldom
have I eaten with such an appetite, and I found the
beefsteak excellent, after being without meat for
so long a time; for some weeks we have had nothing but an occasional partridge; meat, in the
accepted sense of the word, we had only eaten twice
since we left Altar, September 12th, to date,
October 16th, living on beans, a little rice, and as
luck would have it, sixteen pounds of flour we
bought from Mr. Stephenson at the hot springs.
Lieut. Engineer Whipple,[1] now making observa-

---

[1] Amiel W. Whipple, at this time lieutenant of topographical engineers, later made one of the principal Pacific Railroad surveys, and died a major general in 1863 from wounds
received at Chancellorsville. The journal of his expedition
from San Diego to the Colorado was printed as Senate ex. doc.
No. 19, 2d session, 31st Cong. The entry for October 15th,
1849, reads as follows:
"Arrived Colonel Collyer, collector of the port of San
Francisco, escorted by Captain Thorne with thirty dragoons.
Under their protection is also a party of emigrants, com-

tions at the junction of the Gila and Colorado
rivers, was very kind to me, and this evening Col.
Thorn came up with us; we had been expecting
this for some time. Col. Collins [Collier], the
collector from San Francisco treated us with great
courtesy, and I shall reluctantly bid these gentlemen
good-bye, and start across the desert with forty-
six men half mounted, one quarter the rations we
should have had, mules jaded, but the men, thank
God, all in good health.

October 17th. We went only two miles to our
first camp, but today came twelve up the river,
through a cotton-wood bottom; on the road we
heard that Captain Thorn had been drowned.
The canoe in which he was making his last trip,
was capsized, and one of the Mexicans, who could
not swim, seized him in such a manner that he
could not shake him off, nor hold him so as to save
him, and they went down together. So ends the
life of an officer of distinction, whose quiet, gentle-
manly manner won from me my admiration and
good-fellowship during the few hours of inter-
course we had enjoyed.

We passed one or two Indian huts, all Yumas;
they were scarcely friendly, and our trading was
very limited. I saw three about to cross the river,

manded by Mr. Audubon, the younger, naturalist; Lieutenant
Browning, of the navy; Mr. Langdon Haven, and a son of
Commodore Sloat, were with this party, which was suffering
for the want of provisions."

here like the Ohio when it has low banks, but muddy. They had a float of dried rushes on which they put their few garments; the two men stripped without hesitation, but the squaw seemed a good deal put out at our presence; she commenced undoing her sarape two or three times; eventually with a laugh and joke with her companions, she waded into the muddy stream until the water nearly touched her garment, and then with great rapidity and grace removed it, the same instant sinking into the water so quickly, that her person was not in the least exposed; and she swam the river fully as rapidly as her associates.

October 18th. We encamped a few miles further on with nothing for our horses, and morning saw us tramping over dust and sand, to the sand hills twelve miles distant. When we reached them, I mounted one of them to see how our road lay; immediately the rolling sand hills of the Carolina coasts were brought to mind; there was not a tree to be seen, nor the least sign of vegetation, and the sun pouring down on us made our journey seem twice the length it really was.

[*No date.*] We encamped at the wells [Cooke's Wells], and started out at two in the morning to go thirty-six miles to the next grass, having given our animals a good feed of musquit beans, which we found in great abundance, about five miles below us. We went on well until we came to the lagoons, and truly *here* was a scene of desolation. Broken wagons, dead shrivelled-up cattle, horses and mules as well, lay baking in the sun, around the dried-up wells that had been opened, in the hopes of getting water. Not a blade of grass or green thing of any kind relieved the monotony of the parched, ash-colored earth, and the most melancholy scene presented itself that I have seen since I left the Rio Grande.

We turned to our road at twelve o'clock, the sun blazing down on us, and expecting to go nine miles more without water; I feared the mules would never do it, but about two miles further on, we came to good water, and after a short rest on we went for seven more, when we found shade, and a good supper, for the Sergeant's guard here had killed a wild cow, and made us a present of part of it. The thirty-six miles had been made, and the worst part of the road was past.

[*No date.*] Here we stayed one day to wait for some of our party, who had waited hoping to purchase provisions; they were sorely jaded, but had not lost a mule when they re-joined us. Leaving them to rest, I went to Col. Collins' camp for fifty pounds of biscuit and some rice, and we then took the way west, for the next water-hole, our horses loaded with grass; which as it had been good, we had taken the precaution to secure before we started at four o'clock.

[*No date.*] We camped at a pretty lake, shallow but clear, and good to drink; at the back was one of those peculiar rocky mountains so common in this country, and I made an outline of it. Some wagoners killed an ox, but to me it was uneatable, so I turned in as usual, on bread and beans, and the luxury of a cup of tea. Bachman lost his mules here, and he and Walsh stayed until daylight, the rest of us leaving much earlier. I have felt rather anxious about Bachman as he is not strong.

October 23d. San Felipe.[1] Three days of sunny road, and three nights of freezing cold, have brought us to San Felipe, and a pretty valley it is, but no water, and no wood of any consequence, still there is enough for travellers' purposes, and the sight of the trees gave us great pleasure, after the dearth of vegetation through which we have been passing. We find no food here, and most of the company have gone to Santa Isabella, a rancho fifteen miles distant, where they expect to get all we want.

San Felipe. October 24th. My own mules having been more heavily laden than the average,

---

[1] The Indian village of San Felipe has disappeared from the modern map but the name is borne by a creek in this valley. The journey from the Colorado to San Diego is described in Bartlett's *Personal Narrative*, and the itinerary is given in Marcy's *Prairie Traveler* (New York, 1859). An edition of the latter book, disguised as Burton's *Handbook of Overland Expeditions*, was issued in London in 1863.

were very tired, and I have stayed here, leaving
Mess 6, consisting of Joseph Lambert, Ayres, Weed
and Steele five miles behind to wait for Bachman
and Walsh.   The rest started with John Stevens
in charge, for Santa Isabella.   I ascended the first
hill, and had a view of the long rows of cotton-
woods bordering the irrigating ditches of the once
highly cultivated, but now deserted, Mission
grounds.   Desolation reigned everywhere, decayed
stumps of gigantic trees planted by hand, indica-
tions of shrines, from the clumps of beautiful
cedars by which they are so frequently surrounded,
and other tokens of industry, told of the comfort
that had formerly been enjoyed in this lovely
valley.   The hills to the east are all bare, but those
to the west have many beautiful live oaks, running
up the deep ravines that are between each sharp
ridge.

[*No date.*]   As we rode up the valley, entering
the mountains, the contrast between the scene
before us, and the desert we had just left, was like
coming into Paradise, and we trotted along the
banks of a clear little brook, and sauntered on
through patches of wild sage and wild oats, the
first we had seen, with real pleasure.   As we
reached the top of the ridge, one of those beautiful
natural parks, to be seen only in our southern
latitudes, was before us, and we had the first glimpse

of what might be called California; the pleasure I felt then is and will be a lasting one.

Passing the dividing line, we began our descent following another stream, adorned on both sides with the most magnificent California oaks and sycamores; not so excessively large, but of splendid form and broad spreading shade and foliage, in full tropical luxuriance. At sundown, far down the valley of Santa Maria, we rejoined our camp, and found all well, and Mr. Browning treated me to a pound or two of most delicious grapes. They tasted so refreshing and delicious, that for a few minutes I forgot everything else, all my anxieties for the termination of our long and tedious journey, with the attendant troubles and difficulties seemed smoothed over.

[*No date.*] We arrived today at Santa Maria itself, twenty miles further on our way, really enjoying our march through this beautiful valley.

San Diego Mission. November 3d. We spent the night at Santa Maria and then left for San Diego; the country contains many lovely valleys, and some of the hills are beautiful, and richly covered with wild oats, possessing all but water and wood to make it a most desirable land for the farmer. At sundown we reached the Mission of San Diego,[1] once evidently beautiful and com-

---

[1] Charles Franklin Carter's *Missions of Nueva California* (San Francisco, 1900), gives a good description of the present

fortable; its gardens still contain many palms, olives and grapes, and no doubt the plain below, when irrigated, must have been most productive.

We found an American soldier in charge, and as the last reflection of sunlight tipped the waves of the Pacific Ocean with gold, and the sullen roar of the breakers borne in on the last of the sea breeze for that day came to my ears, tired and sad, I sat on the tiled edge of the long piazza leaning against one of the brick pillars in a most melancholy mood. I could remain here a long time musing on what is before me, realizing in the desertion of all about me that all things mortal pass, but it is necessary to continue our journey, as we are six miles from anything to eat, and we know that two long hours will be requisite to get over the distance; so we must go.

San Diego. November 4th. Mr. Browning on his fine horse "Ures" led the way, and I came close at his heels on my favorite mule. Nine o'clock brought us to this town; no hotel nor boarding house, so we went to the quartermaster, Lieut.

---

condition of the mission buildings of California. Under the inspiration of Charles F. Lummis, the "Landmarks Club" of Los Angeles has undertaken the work of repairing and preserving their ruins. See also *Missions of California*, by Laura Bride Powers, (New York, 1897) and *In and Out of the Old Missions of California*, by George Wharton James (Boston, 1905).

Murray,[1] to leave our things and find a place to put our horses. He received us most kindly, his wife setting before us some excellent venison, and the first real bread and butter we had seen since we left New Orleans, to all of which we did complete justice. The Lieutenant apologized for not giving me a bed, following this up by the presentation of a pillow, and regrets that he could do nothing better than this and his floor. I had my blankets and was soon comfortably asleep under the first roof I had slept under since we departed from Jesus Maria.

Lieut. Ord[2] lay next me, and this morning left for the steamer bound for San Francisco, and I went to the office for letters, but found none, so set to work to get provisions ready for the company.

Five miles from San Diego is the bay, beautiful enough on one side, but opposite are long islands of flat land, and the view ends in distant hills far below, no doubt the coast line. Here I saw many old acquaintances among the birds, the brown pelican wheels and plunges for his prey, as on the Gulf of Mexico, terns, curlews (the long-billed),

---

[1] Edward Murray, at this time a lieutenant, resigned from the service in 1855, and was afterwards an officer in the Confederate army.

[2] Edward O. C. Ord (1818-1883), at this time a first lieutenant, later a major general in the Civil War. His long and distinguished service gives his name a place in every American cyclopaedia and biographical dictionary.

the California black-bellied plover, and great numbers of the horned grebe. I killed two of them, and left them with Mr. Murray, as I carried my gun when I went to the fort for our provisions, which were stored in old hide warehouses. The traffic in hides and jerked beef has been for many years the great industry at this place.

I rode on to our camp in the rain, the first we had had for some weeks, and though now cold, and chilling us to the bone, we would have given worlds for it a short time previously, whilst crossing the dreary desert.

CHAPTER VI

San Diego. November 6, 1849. We started for Los Angeles at ten this morning, leaving behind Havens, Sloat, Watkinson, Lee, Snider, Perry, Dr. Trask, Steele, Bachman, Stevens and Cree, to follow by boat; Cree remained at my request to take care of Stevens, who is seriously ill, and Bachman is not strong enough to march further.

The road from San Diego is a pleasant one; northwest over a few moderate hills brings the traveller to the edge of a large bay, which from its appearance seems to be shallow; to the west, mountains, not the Coast Range, and a few miles along this bay, a beautiful "hollow" rather than valley, opens, and after six or eight miles leads to some steep and disagreeable hills, where our first night from San Diego will be passed. I did not regret leaving San Diego, except for the kindness received there (it is a miserable Mexican town) and our own rather forlorn condition. About forty men continue with me, half of us on foot, the other half scarcely much better, as our animals are woefully jaded, but we could not stop, for we are even worse off for funds than for mounts, as we have only about four hundred dollars, for all our expenses, for over six hundred miles. But our outlay will be small, for with all the assistance of the officers, which has been most liberally given, we have only secured half rations of flour and pork; we are so accustomed to doing without sugar and coffee, that we scarcely care for it.

November 7th. We were off at daylight according to custom, and followed the trail over hill and hollow, with an occasional valley. At times the ocean was in full view, its soft blue horizon line melting into the clear, cloudless sky. To our right, high over the Mission of St. Louis del Rey, smiled, glistening in snowy purity, the highest peaks of the Snowy Mountains, Sierra Nevada. The soil is black loam, and the bottoms still blacker, but on this day's travel much of the soil has been salt.

Seeing a few ducks alight at a little lake, almost like a running stream, I went after them, and found some hundreds of gadwalls, and bald-pates, and in half an hour had sufficient for all our company, which I need not tell you we enjoyed, though not cooked at Baltimore "à la Canvasback."

Hundreds of California marmots are seen daily, at a distance looking like a common squirrel, so much so that the men all call them squirrels; their color varies very much, being every shade of grey and reddish brown.

The Mission of Luis Rey,[1] as it is now called, now in the possession of the Americans, is kept by an old Mexican; it presents, as you get the first view of it going north, one of the most impressive scenes I can recall; its long row of low, but regular arches, the façade whitewashed, and the church at the east end, with many outlying buildings covered with red tiles, the whole standing in a broad valley running eastward for miles, until the view ends in the snowy peaks of the Sierra Nevada, compels the traveller to pause and to admire.

As we stood looking at all this, from a hill higher than the one on which we were, swooped a California vulture, coming towards us until, at about fifty yards, having satisfied his curiosity, though not mine, he rose in majestic circles high above us, and with a sudden dash took a straight line, somewhat inclining downwards, towards the mountains across the valley and was lost to sight, from actual distance.

The garden of the Mission has been beautiful, and we found it still well stocked with vines, olives, figs, etc., but the same desolation is visible everywhere through this country of splendid soil, which here is rather sandy. There is still lack of wood and water, irrigation has been universal.

---

[1] San Luis Rey was reoccupied and a Franciscan college established there in 1893.

The Missions seem to have been divided into the residence, with beautiful gardens, the church, the stock farm and the grain-growing lands, and all have possessed much comfort if not considerable wealth. Naturally those who lived in them wished to isolate themselves from the world, and to surrender the pleasures and ambitions found there, for the advancement of their religion, or, at least, were willing to do so.

November 9th. I have already seen the nucleus of an American rancho, in this country, which is lonely rather than desolate. We have passed many fine old Missions, at least six or seven, but though in the midst of beautiful land, with hundreds of horses and cattle, and many herds of sheep and goats, the indolence of the people has left all decaying, and they live in dirt and ignorance, and merely vegetate away this life in listlessness, except for the occasional excitement of a trade in horses, or a game of monte. We have had many melons, late in the season as we are; they are pulled and put up as the French do pears, and keep fresh for many weeks.

All the people here ride well, and fast, many without saddles; these latter tie a rope, or if they have it, a surcingle, buckle that around the body of the horse, and stick both knees under it, so that it is a great assistance to them. The gallop is the usual gait at which they travel. The continual absence of wood gives an appearance to all the hills, of old fields, but many of the valleys are truly beautiful; fine sycamores, oaks and cotton-woods along the water making everything look refreshing to a degree that none can realize but those who have been for weeks exposed to sun and rain, keen winds and cold nights, without woods for shelter or fire; in cooking we have often had to keep up a fire with weeds, some men attending to this, while the others fried our meat, made coffee, and what we *called* bread.

Los Angeles. This "city of the angels" is anything else, unless the angels are fallen ones. An antiquated, dilapidated air pervades all, but Americans are pouring in, and in a few years will make a beautiful place of it. It is well watered by a pretty little river, led off in irrigating ditches like those at San Antonio de Bexar. The whole town is surrounded to the south with very luxuriant vines, and the grapes are quite delightful; we parted from them with great regret, as fruit is such a luxury to us. Many of the men took bushels, and only paid small sums for them.

The hills to the north command the whole town, and will be the place for the garrison.

San Pedro, twenty-seven miles south-west, is the port, and is *said* to have a good harbor. All the country round is rolling, and in many places almost mountainous. Before you get to the Coast Range

the soil is most of it very good, and the cattle are
fine; wild mustard grows everywhere, to the
height of five feet or more; in the richest soil
attaining seven and eight feet, and we have twice
cooked our meal with no fuel but the stalks of this
weed.

We have had great trouble with our mules for
want of grass, and the poor things wandered miles,
and we lost some few, and had difficulty in getting
the others. After long consultations we decided
to divide, eleven of us to bring on the mules and
take the valley of the Tulare for our route; the
rest of the company under Henry Mallory going
up in the barque Hector for thirty dollars each, as
our mules are utterly broken down, and we want
to get them through to San Francisco if we can.
So much for our splendid outfit, so much for the
plans of our Military Commander. But let it pass,
and I will try to describe our route.

[*No date.*] Leaving Los Angeles at one o'clock,
with forty-six mules and ten men, I making the
eleventh, and two of the number being my true
friends Browning and Simson, we passed eastward
of the town, and followed the little river of the
same name, and camped on the best grass we had
had, and with so good a beginning, expected to
have the same for our poor animals for the rest of
our journey, and in some degree recruit them and
heal their sore backs.

[*No date.*] Today our ride of about eighteen miles was over a plain of rather poor soil, and we found the rancho; it was formerly the Mission of San Fernando.[1] Like most of the others, it has a long portico and arches; a few pictures of the Virgin and some images of the saints are still standing, but, from an artistic point of view, they are poor trash. The garden is still most luxuriant, and many grapes are grown here, and wine made, as well as other liquors distilled. It looked like sacrilege to me to see the uses made of sacred places but so the changes appear to be in these countries; dilapidation immediately follows the removal of the priests. Great dislike was manifested to the Americans here, and they would neither give nor sell any of the fruits they had in such abundance, grapes and melons wasting on the ground.

Leaving this rancho we camped five miles further on our way, up an arroyo, in tall, rush-like grass, where we had only bad water, being so charged with sulphur and various salts as to be undrinkable. The hills are of a friable, whitish clay and sandstone, and after a very steep ascent, we gradually descended into a beautiful valley to the rancho San Francisco, and encamped in sight of it with good water, and plenty of wood. In the

[1] San Fernando is, of all the missions of California, in the best condition. Its two principal buildings are in a good state of preservation and the church has been re-roofed by the "Landmarks Club."

morning Rhoades killed the first black-tailed deer
that any of the party has secured. We found it
very good meat, and quite enjoyed it, after the
continuance of beef we have had since our arrival
on this side of the great divide, as at the rancho we
can usually buy fine, young cattle for from eight to
twelve dollars.

[*No date.*] We now commenced the regular
ascent of the Coast Range, the mountains at first
were sandy loam and sandstone; we had no grand
views, even of distance, and we lost two of our
mules from fatigue. Our descent was rapid for
some miles, and brought us to the gorge leading to
the dividing ridge, where was a rapid torrent,
about up to our knees, and as we followed it scenes
of the wildest description presented themselves.
Sometimes it looked as if our further progress was
completely at an end, and again a turn at right
angles showed us half a mile more of our road.
The rocks here are shelly sandstone, looking at
first sight, at a distance, like slate. The tops of all
the mountains are covered with snow, and the wind
from the northwest was blowing so hard as to bring
our tired mules to a standstill, as the puffs struck
them.

As we came out into the plain or valley a few
squalls of hail and rain came on, and we were glad
to camp near some cottonwoods, not deeming it
prudent to be under them, as their limbs had

already, some of them, yielded to the mountain gusts and fallen.

[*No date.*] *Tulare Valley.* One more day brought us to this great valley, and the view from the last hill looking to northwest was quite grand, stretching on one hand until lost in distance, and on the other the snowy mountains on the east of the Tulare valley. Here, for the first time, I saw the Lewis woodpecker, and Steller's jay in this country. I have seen many California vultures and a new hawk, with a white tail and red shoulders. During the dry season this great plain may be travelled on, but now numerous ponds and lakes exist, and the ground is in places, for miles, too boggy to ride over, so we were forced to skirt the hills. This compelled us sometimes to take three days when two should have been ample. Our journeys now are not more than twenty miles a day, and our nights are so penetrating and cold, that four blankets are not too many.

[*No date.*] Our morning's ride, as we had anticipated, was pleasant after the hills, but not directly on our course, as the late rains had made the soil, always soft, impassable for our mules, from the mud. We wound round the mountains for about twenty-five miles, to the first Indian village we had seen, though we had passed several single huts. Being far ahead of the train, I had time to look at their household style of living, and saw them grinding their acorns, and fanning grass and other seeds, so as to prepare their winter's food. They appear to make a sort of pulp of the acorn by grinding it in a most simple mill of stone, using two kinds as convenience or ownership suggests. One, a standing mill, and the other a kind of mortar and pestle style, the mortar being formed by continual use of the same place, until from two to six inches deep, and if the large stone is favorable, from ten to twelve holes are seen in the same one.

These Indians were friendly and seemed pleased to see Americans coming into the country, and I have no doubt but that their condition will be greatly ameliorated by the change from savage to half-civilized life.

We saw one company already installing themselves in this beautiful valley, where they hope to make permanent homes.

[*No date.*] For two days heavy rolling hills of black soil, clay and gravel with an occasional arroyo of sand, made our journey tedious, but we gradually arrived in better country for travelling, but less grass, and, as we neared the San Joaquin River, immense herds of antelope and elk were seen, so wild that it was difficult to approach them.

[*No date.*] This is our second day on the San Joaquin River, and we have secured a fine elk and

an antelope, three geese and two Sandhill cranes
(I am sure different from ours) so that we have
feasted luxuriously.   Many thousand geese are
seen daily, and we are travelling on cheerfully,
making our twenty-five miles with ease, and camping by half-past four or five o'clock.   After supper
we sit round our camp fires for an hour or so, and
then turn in for the night, to be ready for the
early start on the morrow.

The nights here are in great contrast to the days,
and are exceedingly cold, for all the icy mountains
send their damp air down, as the sun sinks behind
them.

Following down the San Joaquin southwest and
west, we came to the river of the lakes, and stood
off northwest (its general course) for nearly two
days, but were so impeded in our progress by the
bull-rushes that we turned aside to a clump of
trees, where we expected to find water and grass;
but not succeeding, returned to the river, about
eight miles, and with great difficulty reached the
edge of it for water at dusk — cold, tired, and
regretting our lost time.   We resolved, nevertheless, to steer off from the rushes next day.   This is
the locality from which, I suppose, the valley takes
its name, "tulare" meaning "rush," this plant
taking here the place of all others.

[*No date.*]   Today I ran on to a herd of about
a thousand elk; so close was I that I could see their

eyes perfectly; these elk must be greatly harassed by the wolves, which are very numerous, and so bold at night that we have had several pieces of meat, and a fine goose stolen from over my tent door. Their long, lonely howl at night, the cries of myriads of wild geese, as well as Hutchinson's goose (which is very abundant) and the discordant note of the night heron, tell the melancholy truth all too plainly, of the long, long distance from home and friends.

There is no trail but that of wild horses and elk, all terminating at some water-hole, not a sign of civilization, not the track of a white man to be seen, and sometimes the loneliness and solitude seem unending.

The water is beautifully clear now, and is full of fine-looking fish; the large salmon of these rivers is a very sharky-looking fellow and may be fine eating, but as yet we have not been fortunate enough to get one, though several have been shot by Hudson and Simson as they lay in the shallows. The average width of the river here (that is, two days' journey from the mountains) is about eight yards, but as the snows are high up on the mountains, no doubt a great portion of the water is absorbed by the sandy soil it runs through.

Among the oaks the long acorns of two shapes, a good deal like nuts in taste, but still astringent to a disagreeable degree, are plentiful, and we eat a good many of them both roasted and raw, by way of variety, though objecting to the flavor. I have seen one or two nearly three inches long. Out of these acorns the Indians make their "payote," a kind of paste, which they dry, and then put into water in flakes, no doubt to allow the acrid matter to escape.

[*No date.*] *Stockton.* For the last five days we have passed over vast plains of sandy soil and all the recollections of the desert would come upon us, but for our nightly returns to the river. Passing two small rivers, we came to the Stanislaus, and went down it to the ferry, having once tried, unsuccessfully, to cross it. We had to pay a dollar each for about twenty yards, and went on our way to Stockton.

This mushroom town of skeleton houses and tents, with every class of dwelling from log cabin with rush roof, to the simple blanket spread to shelter the hardy miner, is situated like Houston, Texas, on an elevated flat, so level, that the water lying after every shower, makes the mud as deep as I ever saw it on the rich levees of Louisiana in winter. I find the climate much the same as that in Louisiana, but without the beautifully luxuriant vegetation of that country, and from all accounts it is quite as healthy, except that the high mountains here give a pleasant retreat in summer from the diseases incident to that season.

I left the men at the "French Camp," the first prairie out of the water, five miles to the south-west, and came into Stockton, with Hudson and Boggs and a pack mule to take out provisions for those at the camp. We went into the "Exchange Hotel," which might better be called the "Exchange of Blacklegs." Such a crowd as the bar-room of this hotel presents nightly, cannot be found except where all nations meet. Cards were being played for stakes every where, and the crowd around added to the picture, which once seen is difficult to forget. The tall, raw-boned Westerner, bearded and moustached like his Mexican neighbor beside him, the broad-headed German and sallow Spaniard, French, Irish, Scotch, I know not how many nationalities are here represented. I saw even two Chilians with their cold, indifferent air, all mixing together, each man on his guard against his fellow-man. The tight fitting jacket and flowing sarape touch each other, all blending into weirdness in the dim light of a few candles, would that I had time and opportunity to sketch some of the many scenes I beheld.

Having bought what we required we made our way back to camp through the dark dismal night, wind blowing and rain falling in torrents.

[*No date.*] Today we went up to Stockton again, the approach is through mud and mire, or rather water, reminding one of that at Houston

from the south; the mud, if anything, more disagreeable to walk through.   One wonders at the
way in which men stay here day after day, gambling going on incessantly.   Of course, the sharpers
and experts get all the money, the poor dupes
continue to put down gold-dust, even though every
boat that leaves takes away professional card-
players, and *they* have to return to the mines to dig.
The craze 'for the mines is beyond all credence;
mechanics refuse sixteen dollars a day, to go to the
mines where half an ounce is the regular gain,
though sometimes ten times that amount.

[*No date.*]   We leave tomorrow for San Francisco; today I made a sketch of the east suburb of
the town, and as a proof of the good intentions of
the people to be honest, and keep up good principles, a gallows is the chief object in the foreground.
It was erected to execute a man for murder and
robbery.

A party here got up a club called the "Hounds,"
at first as a patrol, and were of real service, but
later bad habits crept in, such as knocking up any
bar-keeper at any hour of the night and making "a
night of it."   For some time they paid for this on
the following day, always saying as they went out
"To the charge of the Hounds," but at last the
"charge" became the last of the matter; eventually
thefts were committed, and the thief was convicted
by a regular jury, and sentenced.   The day for his

execution came, and he felt assured that he would
be rescued by his friends, and probably would
have been, but for the arrival of a ship-load of
emigrants, who, on being informed of the fact,
marched out, fully armed, to see the law carried
into effect.

The prices of everything here are beyond belief;

Flour,	$ 40.00 per barrel.
Pork,	65.00 per barrel.
Pilot bread,	.20 per pound.
India-rubber boots,	50.00 to $60.00.
Flannel shirts,	6.00 to $ 8.00.
Shot,	.30 per pound.
Powder,	1.00 to $1.50 per lb.
Government tents,	40.00, at home $12.00.
India-rubber,	100.00.
Freight to the mines,	.50 per pound.

and almost every other article in proportion; for
cleaning my watch and putting on a new crystal,
$16.00. Yet with these high prices scarcely one
becomes rich. Board $3.00 to $6.00 a day, without
lodging. Washing and ironing $6.00 a dozen.

We are in a forlorn condition, almost without
clothes, and our mules broken down, yet wretched
as we are no company coming by land has done
better, and mine is only the second yet holding
together. This shows how honorable the men are,
for [with] wages from $5.00 to $10.00 per day,

and mechanics (of which our company has several) [getting] from $10.00 to $16.00, these men stand by their contract.

[*No date.*] We none of us regret leaving Stockton, where we have been for four days delayed by the steamer, our ill-luck as regards waitings still follows us. We are going in the steamer Captain Southern. [?]

San Francisco. December 23d. The day we left Stockton we had one of the most violent gales I had seen for many a week, and our boat, a little steam side-wheeler, was so flat and so light that the strong wind from the south-east had us ashore twenty times in the first hour, on the banks of the slough which leads to the San Joaquin, the main stream leading to the upper bay, Suisun; finally anchors and all were dragged high on the bulrushes, and we were delayed two days more.

We reached San Francisco on Saturday night December 21st, and stayed in our blankets on the floor of the steamer until morning when we went off, on what is called "the long dock" into mud half-leg deep. We paid fifty cents for a cup of coffee and a bit of bread, and I went for my letters, but found none, so went off to hunt up my men, found them all right, and returned to Henry Mallory, who having received letters was able to set my anxieties about my family at rest; but I alone of all the company had no home news. I sat on

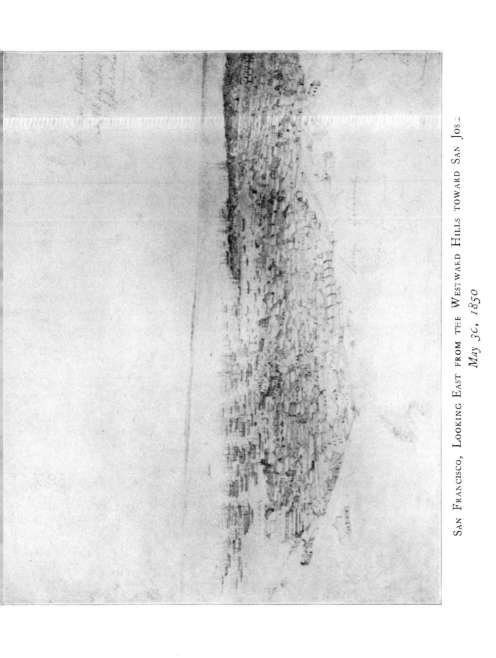

SAN FRANCISCO, LOOKING EAST FROM THE WESTWARD HILLS TOWARD SAN JOSÉ
May 30, 1850

the deck of the steamer, the most quiet place I could find, re-read my old letters, and went about my business with a heavy heart.

San Francisco. December 25th 1849. Christmas Day! Happy Christmas! Merry Christmas! Not that here, to me at any rate, in this pandemonium of a city. Not a *lady* to be seen, and the women, poor things, sad and silent, except when drunk or excited. The place full of gamblers, hundreds of them, and men of the lowest types, more blasphemous, and with less regard for God and his commands than all I have ever seen on the Mississippi, [in] New Orleans or Texas, which give us the same class to some extent, it is true; but instead of a few dozen, or a hundred, gaming at a time, here, there are thousands, and one house alone pays one hundred and fifty thousand dollars per annum for the rent of the "Monte" tables.

Sunday makes no difference, certainly not Christmas, except for a little more drunkenness, and a little extra effort on the part of the hotel keepers to take in more money.

I spent the morning looking over my journal, and regret it has been kept so irregularly, yet, as I read it, and recall my experiences since last March, I wonder that I have been able to keep it at all. I dined with Havens, Mr. McLea, Lieut. Browning and Henry Mallory, and you may be sure home was in our thoughts all the time, even if other topics of conversation were on our lips. It seemed impossible for me to shake off my depression.

December 26th. I was not made more cheerful by finding that our agents had so conducted our affairs that instead of finding all our provisions and implements nicely stored, and in good order, waiting for us, I discovered that all that was most useful to us had been sold, and the balance lay about in the wet and mud, or was rotting, half dry for want of the requisite cover. The expenses had eaten up the money procured by the sales, or so we were told, and I found myself with forty men to take care of and in debt. I was on the point of breaking up the company, and letting every man shift for himself, but felt that it was neither brave nor honorable, so decided to make one more effort. I drew on my brother for one thousand dollars, borrowed all I could from the boys who had brought their own mules on with them, and concluded to take all who were not mechanics with me to the mines; the mechanics had, without exception, found work instantly at exorbitant prices. They were to keep half they made, and pay in the other half to the company. I have been offered thirty-five dollars a day to draw plans for houses, stores, etc., but though I never intended to go to the mines myself, I feel now for the sake of the men who stood by me, that I must stay by them.

My paints and canvas have been left on the desert, my few specimens lost or thrown away; and lack of time, and the weakness produced by my two illnesses at Monterey and Parras, and the monotonous food, have robbed me of all enthusiasm; often I had to force myself to swallow the little I did, knowing I must if I was to get through at all.

Van Horn and Dr. Perry will remain in San Francisco and the men who go up to the mines with me, are Havens, Layton, Hewes, Bloomfield, McGown, Lee, Watkinson, Jno. R. Lambert, Jos. Lambert, J. S. Lambert, Hutchinson, Damon, Jno. Stevens, Cree, Van Buren, Ayres, Hinckley, Jno. Stevenson, Black, Liscomb, Elmslie, E. A. Lambert, Dr. Trask, Steele, Weed, Henry Mallory, Mitchell, Walsh, Valentine, Simson, McCusker, Tone, Hudson, Pennypacker, Clement, Boggs, Lieut. Browning, with myself, thirty-eight in number.

December 29th. We left San Francisco in the same steamer we had travelled on from Stockton. The week's rain over, with the bay like a mirror, and a clear sky over all, it was an enchanting scene. I thought with gratitude of the kindness I had received from Messrs. Chittenden, Edmondson, McLea and many others; not only had they frequently made me their guest, but they had given me most valuable information and advice, in reference to my future proceedings.

As we moved off I could see the whole town situated on high hills facing the bay, to the southeast on one side, to the southwest on the other. I could almost fancy as we made our way to the open bay through the crowd of vessels, that I could hear the chink, chink of dollars as the gamblers put them down on the Monte tables, and a picture of the whole place, a regular Inferno, came before me as plainly as if I actually saw it. Every house, with rare exceptions, letting out their bar-rooms as well as all other available space, for gambling purposes, immense rents being paid for a mere shell of a house. In some of the hotels one hundred dollars a day was paid for space to place a single Monte table; but I will leave all this, and sail on over the beautiful bay towards the east, which sends the gold that makes this hell-hole of crime and dissipation.

Passing out of the mass of shipping to the left, opens out the pass to the ocean, and ahead of us, surrounded by beautiful hills, smooth but steep, green and velvety to look upon, a few tall redwoods ended the view to the south. The water was as smooth as a lake, and the moon rose on so calm a sheet that its reflection was a long, straight line of light, almost as brilliant as itself, and I sat late on the deck to admire it, and to think of all at home, but at last went down to the filthy cabin, wrapped myself in my blankets and lay down in a corner possibly a shade less dirty than the others.

We reached Stockton, and after a day in the mud I found my goods stored safely and all ready for packing, Mr. Starbuck to whom I had entrusted them having been most faithful. We went to the hotel for supper which was worth, perhaps, ten cents, but cost a dollar and a half each. After which, with Browning, Simson, Stevens, Bloomfield and some of the others, I took a look up and down the town. The gambling was going on as usual, the tables had changed hands in some instances, but the many are still sitting behind their "banks." A young English nobleman, who asked me to keep his name a secret, laughed and said: "We are all *bankers* here." One young man, too young for such work, terrible at any age, I felt sorry to see; he had evidently been a winner to judge from the large amount before him, having a wall of gold dust ounce high and three rows deep, leaving a space of nearly a foot square inside, well filled with gold pieces of all stamps and countries, the 16, 8 and 4 of the Spanish, the eagles and half-eagles of the United States, sovereigns and half sovereigns of England, and others from apparently all over the world, lumps even of unalloyed gold, had all fallen into his hands today. He seemed quite alone; his candles were still burning, and he rested his cheek on a delicate, well formed hand, which looked as if it had not been made for the shovel and pick of the mines. He

was a very handsome young fellow, I should judge
from Virginia, with a profusion of half curling
light hair and deep grey eyes. Suddenly he rose,
looked about him, and said in a quivering voice:
"Well, I came here to make my fortune, I've made
it, there it is, but, Oh God, how can I face my
mother." He burst into tears and dashed from
the room, which for an instant was in absolute
stillness. Two men came up, spoke to the banker
[?] in low tones, swept the gold into two canvas
bags and followed the youth, or so I presume.

CHAPTER VII

A TOUR OF THE GOLD-FIELDS

January 2d, 1850. Leaving Stockton we tramped through .mud and water, so like the coast of Louisiana (the Mississippi) that it might have been winter there, instead of in California. We had packed the day before leaving, so left early for our walk of twenty miles after our pack-mules, and went over a partially sandy prairie to the Stanislaus River, and at eight that night reached good wood and water, and encamped about three miles from the river. Next morning, January 3d, we left in the rain for the ferry, but owing to the bad weather, heavy roads and exhaustion of Bachman and McGown, stopped at a good camping ground, with excellent grass, after going only three miles. The rain poured all day and all night, and we lost two days here in consequence, for the river rose so rapidly that we could not cross our mules. The next day the most of us did get over, and Clement and Hudson remained behind to look after the mules.

January 6th. Leaving the middle ferry, known as Islip's, our first day was over a good road with occasional quicksands in the way. The next day,

January 7th, 1850, as we had a cold northeast drizzle, we lay by, and the following morning, January 8th, left for our destination, the Chinese Mines.   Many of the views before us, as we mounted hill after hill looking towards the mountains, are very beautiful park-like country; the roads are a series of mud-holes and quicksands at this season, and the trees, either swamp, or post-oak, with occasionally a fine ridge of a species of live-oak.   At times we had to pack the cargoes of the weaker mules, every few hundred yards, and at one place, had nine mules mired at the same time, the mud being so tenacious that even when the packs were taken off, the poor animals could not get out without our help.   Three days of such travelling brought us to our present camp, the soil red clay and sand, mixed thinly with white quartz of various sizes, but generally small, not more than two, or at most, three inches in diameter, and generally even smaller.

[*No date.*]   We went up to the "diggings"[1] on the morning after our arrival, and looked round to see what prospects were ahead of us.   We found the little branches bored, and pitted, and washed

---

[1] There is a map of the mining camps in H. H. Bancroft's *History of California*, vol. vi, pp. 368-369.   Topographical details are given in the "Claim" sheets, issued by the United States Geological Survey.   The inset in the map of Audubon's route, at the end of this volume, is intended to locate only the places visited by him.

out in every direction, so much so that we tried to
"prospect" for ourselves, and we lost three days.
We found the men already there kind and polite,
showing the mode of working and washing, of
digging and drawing most willingly, and tomorrow open a pit close beside some of the most
fortunate.

The uncertainty of digging renders the life of
the miner, for profit, that of a gambler, for most
of his good luck depends on chance. At times you
may see two pits side by side, one man getting two
ounces a day, and the other hardly two dollars:
we heard of one instance of much greater disparity;
two friends working next each other found that at
the end of the week, one had an ounce of gold,
worth about twenty dollars, the other gold worth
six thousand dollars. So it goes, and we shall all
have to work hard. Again and again I am over-
whelmed by the thought that I am at these dreary
mines — I, who started intent on drawing and
obtaining new specimens — to have so different a
destiny thrust upon me, is bewildering.

The ground here is beautiful rolling valley of
sandy clay, so like the post-oak country of Texas
that one might almost fancy himself there. A few
pines are scattered about, the cones are very large,
say six inches long, and three in diameter; the seed
is a pleasant nut, about the size and shape of a
small, shelled almond; the quantity of resin con-

tained is very great, and at the end of every leaf of the cones, quite a lump is seen.

The ultramarine jay, and Steller's, the red-shafted woodpecker and California quail are abundant, and many finches, some new, and others that I know, are everywhere; but I have no time to skin and preserve specimens.   Then too, the black-tailed deer, California hare, and grizzly bear, are common, as well as the small hare.   There are some few squirrels and a marmot or two, but I have not been able to procure them; I have also seen the robin of this country and many others.   The country is otherwise barren, I wish I was out of it.

January 20th, 1850.   Chinese Diggings.   It does not seem possible, remembering the difficulties of the road, that we are only seventy miles from Stockton.   The men began "rocking" yesterday, one cradle, and get about a dollar an hour, but hope to get more when in the way of it.   Those at work around us get an average of fourteen a day, and at times much more; then again a week's work is lost.   The quantity of gold, so I am told by those who know more of it than I do, is very great, but so diffused that great labor is required to get it.   The lottery of the whole affair is beyond belief.   The richest gulches are supposed to be those on the river, the Tuolome [Tuolumne], or the creeks leading to the river.   The pit, or piece of ground allotted to each man is sixteen feet square, this having been settled by the diggers, and the law is enforced by an alcalde. Many is the week's work, the men say, when they do not get the price of their board, and again large amounts are found. One individual told me he was getting two ounces a day, and gave his claim up, to join a company in digging out the bed of a river which they had drained off. He worked a month at the river scarcely making two dollars a day, while the man who bought his first place, had accumulated several thousands. I have heard fifty such stories, but as a whole this country will pay the laborer and the mechanic better than the miners, unless the latter have capital. Had we come my route and reached here with a hundred mules, a fortune could soon have been made by packing. But, alas! against my better judgment I allowed myself to be swayed by Col. Webb, who had his own way at the cost of twenty-seven thousand dollars, thirteen lives, and the loss of many months to all the men who came through.

Chinese Diggings. February 1st, 1850. Friday, and a most beautiful day; birds all around are in gay chatter, and the song of the raven, jay-like, but sweet to listen to, from the attempt at softness, as he nods and bows with swelling throat to his mate. It is like March in Louisiana. Alas for the poor fellows who have left the southern states to come to this, and settle here as farmers; to be drowned out in winter, and burnt up in summer! However, when the excitement of the gold fever ceases, as it must, California will find its level with the other states, and many a hastily made fortune will be as rapidly lost.

I am leaving for the North Fork of the Stanislaus, twenty-five miles, to make one more effort to keep the company together and to pay off our indebtedness to the stockholders, but I fear my efforts will be useless.

Murphy's Diggings. Sunday, February 10. Everything seems against us — weather and season, water and rain, interrupt us in all our attempts at work, and ill-luck seems to follow us. After fruitless labor at the Chinese Diggings I came here, where the diggings are said to be very rich, but where we have to wait for the waters to subside, perhaps two months, and I have not the means to keep the men for that length of time, even if the date of their contract did not expire before then.

These diggings are said to be the richest in the southern mining district and here I came to make my last effort for the good of my men; for myself my home is awaiting me, and ample means to pay off all the indebtedness I have personally incurred; many times a day I thank God I never asked one man to join the venture, though I feel strongly that some, notably Clement, Walsh, Boden, poor fellow, my cousin Howard Bakewell, and a few

others joined because I did.   Knowing this, and
knowing too how many have risked their all, I
hesitate to leave, as long as I feel I can be of help
in any way, and shall go into the matter very
carefully with the men, most of whom however I
know feel as I do.

February 25th, 1850.   Today we all met together and after much serious talk, I told the men
that their time was more than up, and that, consequently they were their own masters and the company dissolved.   I told them, too, that I was ready
to help each and all to the best of my ability, poor
enough, but I believed we could do better in other
ways than mining.   Not a word was said, and
silently all went to their tents; we had been a year
together, in sickness and trouble, in boisterous
mirth and sorrowful anxiety, and like old and tried
friends we felt the coming separation keenly; we
were all greatly depressed.   I shall be with the men
for some weeks, and shall then try to make up for
part of what I have lost, making drawings and
sketches, and collecting such specimens as I can.   I
am bitterly disappointed for the men who have
been so faithful, and who have stood by me so
staunchly, but as Tone said to me some hours after
our talk: "There's more money to be made here by
land speculations, and every kind of work than
there is in mining, and those who work will get on."
I quite agree with him, and when one hears of the

return of men with large fortunes, ask if speculations in land or trade, bar-keeping or Monte dealing has not swollen the first few hundreds, dug and gained with hard labor, privation, or, in rare cases, wonderful luck. Even then for one man who has a thousand, there are hundreds who will not average a tenth of it after expenses are paid.

March 6th. Again on the road from Stockton east, towards the mines. I have been to San Francisco and am now on my way to join Layton to begin my tour of the mining and agricultural districts of this now most fairy-like country, everything so smiling and beautiful, flowers of the smaller varieties by thousands; and the snow melting sends its waters down all the little rills and rivulets clear and pure, giving freshness and luxuriance to the whole country; could it retain so much beauty through the summer, I should pronounce it, at once, the most enchanting land I had ever seen, and yet, as I think of the beautiful shrubs of the east, and where they do exist, of the magnolias, wild roses, and flowering vines and trees we have, I think the countries balanced, for here two species of oak, three pines, the redwood and the laurel, will almost enumerate the whole of the common varieties of trees.

Farther south, back of San Diego, in the valley of Santa Maria, I saw the finest sycamores I have ever come across; they grow where they have room enough to extend their gigantic limbs laterally, instead of forcing their huge trunks in rivalry with the oaks, to get fresh air and sunshine.

The country from Stockton is a clayey flat, so little of an inclination to the land, that the water appears to lie until evaporated, and the "sloughs" in many places are sluggish and seem to be more water-holes than running streams, until they reach the Calaveras, which is a beautiful creek nearly dry four months of the year, but the other eight giving good water. The meadow-like flats about it look just ready for the plough, though by using that, a sward of good grass would be lost. The country from here becomes very gradually more and more undulating, changing the nature of the soil every few miles. In some places the hills are of clay, and valleys of greyish loam, or red sand thickly mixed in with quartz; in many cases water-worn, but all is so beautiful that were the woods more dense, and the water-courses now so inviting, "never-failing," the farmer would here find his Paradise, and by selecting his land so as to avoid the gravelly sub-soil, which is too abundant for richness, and choosing that which has the clay foundation, his plantation might be one of great permanence, for the rains here do not wash off much of the soil.

March 8th. Following up one of the north forks of the Calaveras, we passed through beauti-

ful valleys, green and luxuriant, but very short
stretches of grass; the hills, at times, so close
together at the base that the valley was almost lost;
but the ascent was rapid, and we found ourselves
soon on the singular hills of this country within
a mile of the Mokolumne [Mokelumne] mines,
where we camped for the night.

March 9th, 1850. The ice this morning was
half an inch thick, and the cold at day-light,
intense. One hour after sunrise, the day began to
be summer, and at nine o'clock our coats were off,
and we were riding towards the beautiful view
made by the interesting lines of Mokolumne hill
and its adjacent fellows, all eccentric, and all interesting.

The soil in the ravines here is mostly clay, but
from time to time partakes of the sandy red clay
so common in this country, resembling very much
the gravelly hills of the post-oaks of Texas. The
ride up the stream to "Mokolumne rich gulch,"
is very interesting, passing between two hills, or
lines of hills, with occasional ravines leading down
to the creek we were following.

We passed an Indian village of six huts; the
squaws were pounding acorns to make "payote,"
in natural mortars, formed by the slight indenta-
tions being used constantly; the pounding of the
stone (small granite boulders, water-worn smooth),
sometimes wear the holes a foot deep; but they

are generally deserted before that depth is reached.
A smooth, flat stone is usually preferred by the
Indians to begin on, and if the country suits their
purposes, and the lodges remain any length of
time in the neighborhood, the stone is often marked
with thirty or forty of these mortar holes.

[*No date.*] Leaving "Rich gulch," we took a
southerly course over the ridge, and wound down
the branches of the Calaveras, until the various
rivulets united and formed what is called the
"north branch of the Calaveras." Where we
crossed, it was about eighteen inches deep, and
runs over a rough bed of various sized pebbles,
with larger lumps of granite and quartz for the
horses to stumble over, making the ford when the
stream is muddy from recent rains, very treach-
erous. The soil is of the same character for a
mile or two, occasionally of a reddish loam, containing both clay and sand, mixed with gravel, of
angular formation, very small, and with more or
less quartz, equally various as to the size and quantity of the pieces.

The pits dug by the miners at the Chinese Diggings, five miles from the Tuolome [Tuolumne]
River, and midway between the mountains and
plains, among the hills, present ordinarily a superficial loam of from six to eighteen inches, rich, at
times, but again of the light bluish clay; the next
stratum is of reddish clay and gravel, and very

hard, ending in slatey rock, soft and dead to pick at, and having the usual friability of the trap slate that is so plentiful all over the country, sticking up in places like the headstones of a deserted churchyard. At Wood's Diggings the same appearance is seen, but with the slate in more upright strata and hard.

March 18th. At Murphy's New Diggings, the gulch is full of lumps of granite and heavy gravel; in the part called "The Flat" in the lower part of the valley the soil is of great depth, in places eight to ten feet, less in others.

March 20th. From Murphy's New Diggings to Angel's Camp is six miles; the country just undulating, inviting the squatter to put up his log house, made from the few pines that, from time to time, form little clusters, but so far apart as always to arrest the attention, and call forth the admiration of the wanderer through these lonely hills, where the want of woods to me gives more solitude than our densest forest; so much for habit, for I recollect well that "Beaver," my Delaware Indian guide in Texas, always was anxious for the prairie, whenever I took him into the deep swamps of the Brasos or Guadaloupe.

"Angel's Diggings" is one of the many repetitions of the same thing seen every day. A beautiful little brook, with precipitous sides, and gravelly or rocky beds; high hills of red clayey loam, mixed

or sprinkled with bits of quartz and slate, forming continual amphitheatres at almost every bend
of the creek. Here I met a gentleman who had,
for many years, been washing gold in the Caro-
linas; he had a quicksilver machine of his own
invention, price one thousand dollars, which he
was working with six men. He told me he was
getting a pound a day from the sands he was washing, which had been washed already in the
common rocker. He did not feel so sure of its
efficacy in the clay diggings, but for sand it certainly was admirable. These diggings like all I
have seen that were worth anything were completely riddled; first by the top washing, and "dry"
washing of the Mexicans, then by the hurried,
superficial "panning out" of the lucky American
who came first and reaped his fortune; next better
dug out by the gold digger for his three ounces
a day, and now toil and hard labor gave the strong
determined washer from small amounts to, occasionally, an ounce a day, when the water will permit him to work.

March 23d. Our road to Cayote [Coyote]
made a "V" from Murphy's, over a poor soil, with
nothing of interest along the six miles but a small
elevation of semi-basaltic sand-stone, mixed with
granite, with large particles of crystal-like spar.

The approach to Cayote is down a red clay hill,
of course, and is on a point made by two little rivers

(I should call them streams) which meet at the lower end of the diggings. The larger one is called the Cayote River, a branch of the north fork of the Stanislaus, and the diggings are about ten miles up if you follow the windings of the creek, but by the road only five to the Stanislaus.

The first year these diggings were worked many large amounts of gold were dug here with little labor; the second year required harder labor for poorer results, and it is its early reputation that keeps it up, though some holes are still paying well; I was told four, out of the fifty then being worked. The largest amount taken in the time I have been here, two days, was found by five Englishmen, two pounds and three ounces; others are well content with an ounce a day and do not give up their holes if much less than that is the result of ten hours or more work.

There are a few Indians near this place; poor, miserable devils, dirty and half clothed, for they have given up buckskin for Mexican blankets, their faces begrimed with dirt and their whole appearance one of neglect and filth. They dig a little gold from time to time and leave a good share of it with a French trader, Poillon by name. He makes his trade pay by giving them presents in the morning to secure their good-will, and a little extra change at night, on his provisions. I saw him selling the lowest part of a leg from the forequarter of a very poor beef at an abominable price, and he turned to me with a pitiful expression, and asked if he ought to let it go for so small a price, showing me an ounce of gold. All Indian trading appears to be done in the same way, make them presents, and then charge double the value of the gift, on the first article they buy.

The food of these Indians is chiefly the "payote" made from the acorns into a kind of gruel, rather astringent to the taste of the white man, but to an Indian digestion all seems good that can be swallowed.

I saw a papoose, too small to walk, with a stone in his hand half as big as his head, shelling out the nuts of the pine-cone, cracking and eating them with the judgment of a monkey, and looking very much like one.

Their wigwams faced the south, and formed an irregular cluster of bark and mud cones; the usual number of fox- and wolf-like dogs gave the same effect that I am accustomed to, but the tribe is not as handsome as the Indians of the east, or even the Yumas, Pimos, or the Maricopas on the Gila.

Leaving Cayote diggings, the trail for five miles passes between two moderately high ridges to Carson's Creek, where the soil changes to a much poorer quality; crossing the creek we ascended a fairly high hill, from which I took a sketch across

the Stanislaus. The sunset effect was fine, but
I had no colors with me.

March 25th. After crossing the Stanislaus we
ascended a long hill leading about southwest,
towards the "Mormon Gulch" three miles distant. The road wound up ravines for the first
two miles, and would have made as beautiful a
walk as it did a ride. All nature was still and
calm, and the silent scene brought Sunday to both
our minds, and we agreed that whether in the
wilderness, or at home, the day brought a feeling
of tranquillity. We almost changed our minds
when we reached the diggings, so different was
the scene. The bar-rooms were all doing a
"thriving business," and the monte dealers were
doing even a better, gloating over the hard-earned
piles of gold dust which ought to have served a
better purpose.

Passing all this, and going up a beautiful
gorge, winding at times so as almost to form a
semi-circle, we turned our course, and came upon
a most exquisite cascade; the water split upon a
bold rock about fifty feet high and tumbled in
leaps of from six to ten feet until it reached the
rocky bed, where it rushed on boiling and bubbling
impetuously until it joined the Stanislaus.

Our walk to Wood's Creek was hot and tiresome,
and after cooling off we took a sponge bath, the
water being too cold for a plunge, and then saun-

tered about looking for the best points at which
to take views of this most beautiful part of the
country. Situated, by comparison, in a basin, and
straggling up and down the creek are here situated
Wood's diggings, Jamestown and Yorktown. The
soil looks poor, and the rock is granite and sandstone with some slate. On the high points and
peaks of "Table Mountain" huge masses of con-
glomerate boulders, two feet and more in diameter,
are scattered everywhere, and give a dreary look
to all the north side of Wood's diggings. The
hill to the west has shot up into beautiful obelisks
of quartz, and you only cease to admire it to be in
raptures over the views seen by turning east, to
look over mountain beyond mountain, snowy peaks
bare of trees, and between them the rounded points
of hills, looking tiny by comparison. To the
south, bold, rounded but high mountains, full of
verdure and with most graceful outlines, enchant
you, while the verdant stretches at the foot of these
mountains have a pastoral air which made us think
of home.

March 27th. My day passed in a vain attempt
to transfer to canvas the scene before our tent;
when I had worked some hours I went into the
tent next to ours, where lies a poor man, ill, pale,
dejected, unable to move even a few steps. His
mud roof leaks, the soil forming the side of his
cabin is so porous that it admits such quantities of

water that a ditch is necessary to carry it off from the dirt floor. This man came round the Horn, and the long voyage and poor food left him such a victim of scurvy that since he arrived in California, the first of last October, he has worked only six days; the relative with whom he came, and who has toiled for both, has only been able to keep them in provisions, with his best endeavors; he has no money to get home, now his only wish. This man is the brother of Barnum, the museum man; he has written to him, and is awaiting a draft which will enable him to return.

Day and night (these beautiful moonlight nights), flock after flock of wild geese pass almost hourly over our heads to the north. I give up in despair trying to fathom the use of their migration, when hundreds of their fellows are known to breed so far south. Their courtship is kept up as they fly high over the grassy plains where they fed last fall, for if you look closely at the flock, you will see that with the exception of the old gander, a fourth larger than the others, as a rule all the rest are in pairs, and the males follow the females so closely that the line is composed of two very near together, two a little distance from them, and so on to the end.

March 28th. Wood's diggings having given me such sketches as I could take, we took the valley road to Chinese diggings, en route for

Hawkin's [Hawkins's] bar, on the Tuolomne. We were assured before we left that "Woods" now only giving five dollars at the most to good workers, once gave as many ounces, and is now kept up on its past reputation by the storekeepers, as all prospectors must pay something; one takes a drink, another some fresh meat, another a pair of boots; all is sold at exorbitant prices, and storekeepers get rich if no one else does. We are now leaving Layton for Sonora Camp, and I, for Hawkin's Bar.

Every turn gives some vista of beauty in this Garden of Eden; the soft southerly breeze is perfumed with the delicate odor of millions of the smaller varieties of prairie flowers, in some places so abundant as to color acres, whole hillsides, so thickly as to hide the ground, and my mule had to eat flowers rather than grass. One without home ties might well feel all his days could be passed in the beauties of these valleys, roseate yellow and blue, so soft that the purest sky cannot surpass the color for delicacy. Tangled masses of vines climb everywhere, hiding the hard surfaces of the quartz rocks, and beyond this exquisite vegetation always some view, wild and impressive, meets the eye.

But to facts: Bob Layton says: "Don't bring your wagons through Chinese Diggings;" and I agree with him, unless you have nine yoke of pretty good oxen to your load of three thousand five hundred pounds. I believe that teams such as these do get about three miles a day across the boggy flat and post-oak quicksands of these diggings. (In many places the body of the luggage wagon is six inches deep in the mud.) This condition lasts from December to March inclusive.

What this country must be in summer I cannot say, but if it cracks as the soil does south of Los Angeles, it must indeed be miserable, and the stories of the Mexicans we met below the Colorado must be true, when they said it was almost impassable.

A few miles on towards Hawkin's Bar on the Tuolomne the country is very fine, and little plains and valleys fill the six miles, all but the last one, which is a steep descent, short and rugged, over clay and rocks. On this ridge the grass is sparse, and "arrow-wood" was plentiful. The day's march over, you set up your tent, and find cool and delicious water from the Tuolomne just as it leaves its mountain gorge; a little creek on the left which has taken its rise below the altitude of snow is twenty degrees warmer, and so more welcome for bathing purposes.

March 29th. The Tuolomne here, one mile above Hawkin's Bar, comes out of a gorge in the hills, which is both steep and rocky, and sends forth the troubled stream to be tossed and dashed over rocks and shallow bars, for miles through

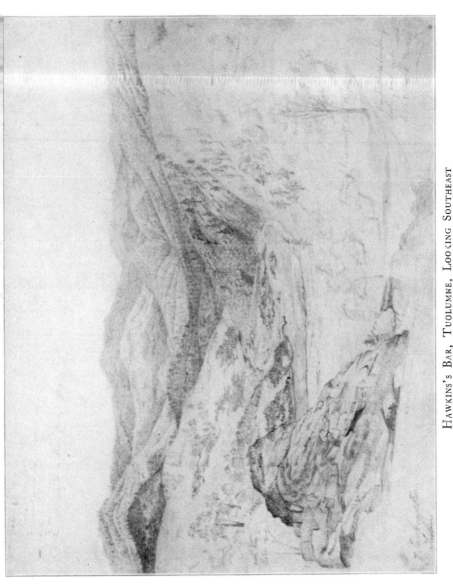

HAWKINS'S BAR, TUOLUMNE, LOOKING SOUTHEAST
April 1, 1850

hills and chasms until it reaches the plains, when it moves quietly, but still rapidly at this season, as it makes its way to the San Joaquin, ninety or a hundred miles from the mouth of that stream.

The river here rises and falls daily and nightly almost with the regularity of the tide, not ordinarily more than a foot or two, this being due to the effect of the sun on the snows of the mountains; the warmer the day the higher the water. At night many men in parties of from twenty-five to fifty are here engaged in digging canals to drain the bed of the river at low water. I learn however that they are greatly hindered in this by numerous springs in the bottom of the river, and though there is no doubt a great deal of gold, the difficulties of getting it without machinery are more than can be realized by any one who has not been here and tried.

The buzzards in this upper country are just pairing. I have seen three or four couples of the California vulture but have not secured one yet.

The bar which was dug here last year is now under water, but I am told it was very profitable and many made five or six thousand from their summer's work. There are many here waiting for the plains to dry and snows to melt, when Hawkin's celebrated bar may again be worked. While I am here, I may as well try to give an idea of how the work is done. When a spot has been selected the digger opens a pit, ordinarily four to six feet deep, but sometimes only the top soil has to be removed before the digger can commence washing; this depends on whether he comes to soil tenacious enough to hold the gold, and keep it from sinking down through light, sandy, or porous soils, until it meets with a formation which prevents it from going deeper into the earth. Sometimes in such places are found large deposits called "pockets," and doubtless there are still many to be discovered. When suitable soil is found the digger takes a panful for washing, and with doubt and anxiety goes to the nearest water to see if his "hole" will pay. He stirs the earth and sand in his pan around, until all the soluble part floats off over the sides of the pan, which is kept under water; he then begins shaking backwards and forwards with a regular movement what is left in his pan, to settle what gold is in it; the gold sinks and all the lighter gravel is tipped to the sides, and the gold is quite below all except the black sand, so like emery that when the gold is very fine it is a great drawback, and difficult to separate. Should the digger find gold enough to warrant his washing the clay at the bottom of his pit, and thereby gaining half an ounce a day he goes on washing, but grumbles at his hard luck, hoping that as he gets deeper in his hole he will get richer also, and that when he comes to rock, he may find a "pocket." The cradle is set up, the water poured over, and the monotony of the digger's life begins, a sort of voluntary treadmill occupation, until homesick and tired, even if successful, he ties up his wallet which contains his wealth, secretes it about his body, and tramps off. A man who is usually successful, and there are not so many, may have acquired five or six thousand dollars, but he has usually aged ten years.

April 5th. Leaving Hawkin's Bar for Green Springs, we sauntered along the trail under the beautiful post-oaks, just now in their greatest beauty, with leaves half-grown and pendant catkins. Now we shot a partridge or a hare, or stopped to let "Riley," our pack mule, luxuriate in some little patch of rich grass, in which he stood knee deep. Overhead we saw the heavy, sweeping motion of the vulture's wing, or watched his silent circles. Around us are flowers innumerable, brilliant, soft, modest, fragrant, to suit all fancies, till, having finished our eight-mile journey, the sun began to cast its evening light over the landscape, for we had started late. Layton had rejoined me, and we set up our tent and I made a sketch.

April 6th. Four o'clock found us on our way back to Hawkin's, to meet a friend of Layton's, N. Howard, who was to be our companion. It was cloudy but beautiful, and at Wedgewood's tent we found our friend, and shelter, of which we were glad, as rain was beginning to fall and soon came down in torrents, swelling the little brook near the tents to a roaring stream.

April 8th. After being delayed by rain, our trio started for Don Pedro's Bar, eight miles down the Tuolomne. The country to look at is most beautiful, and our short walk was one of pleasure and admiration.

April 9th. This morning we crossed the river and after a trot of about five miles came to the cañon. I made my way to the lower end called Indian Bluff and my sketch was finished by probably five o'clock; but having no watch I cannot tell. Here I saw the nests of the California vulture, but on the opposite side of the river, now an impassable torrent.

The country on the south side of this river, where we are, is very hilly, the soil tolerable, and the trees still post-oak. We leave for Stockton tomorrow.

April 10th. The road was pleasant on our way back to Green Springs and for a mile further, and when evening came we pitched our "line" tent, and commenced cooking our supper. We had a California hare, a mallard and a plover, all killed out of season, but food we must have. Howard boasted of his coffee, Layton is the baker of the mess, whilst I parboiled my slices of pork to rid it of its coarse flavor, fried out the lard, and have turned and re-turned the loin and hindlegs of our hare. "Riley" safely tethered near us had an equally good supper of the grass and flowers that were to be his bed, and we spread our blankets and went to sleep, or rather the other two have done so, and I, writing by the firelight, shall soon follow their example.

April 11th. Our road today was almost the same that I had travelled with the company going from Stockton to Chinese Camp or diggings, but how changed the scene. The road then was soft mud and mire for miles; now it is as hard as brick, and the hills then scarcely tinged with green by the early sprouting vegetation are now fresh and beautiful with every shade of green and brilliant flowers of all colors. At every rise of ground we paused and turned to look back at the range of the Sierra Nevada softening and mellowing in the hazy light of the sun, the brilliancy enhanced by the deepening blue of the distant hills which form the last outline on the eastern horizon.

Here I tried my hand again at oil painting for landscape, but can only blot in what will answer hereafter to give me local color. After painting about three hours we packed up and started again, as there was no water near us, and took our direction westerly. We found the beds of the streams that in January were beautiful little rivulets, now bright sand bleaching in the sun, their waters dried up or only a tiny trickle. As we descended from one table land to another the rich vegetation became broken by spots of barrenness, and at times whole plains of weeds, not strong and rank showing fertile land, but coarse, noxious, ungainly with disgusting smell, extended for three or four miles and we followed the dusty road almost feeling that we were again on our terrible journey through Mexico last summer.

All these valleys along the river look more fertile in winter than at this season, as the wet and moisture gives the appearance of richness, which is now completely dissipated by the already parched-up effect of the land.

To give you some little idea of the changes occurring in this country: the ferry we crossed last winter (and could only be taken over after great bargaining for a dollar each), we crossed today, all three of us, and our mule for the same sum of one dollar. So at the mines, the same change has taken place; last year an ounce was considered the average of the produce of good working men per diem; this year half an ounce is considered the average, by equally good and better skilled workmen. The people at home will not believe that the roads are travelled by a continuous line of miners; some on foot, some with packs, mules, wagons, in search of "better luck."

The snows are melting so fast just now that the river is within two feet of being as high as when I crossed in the winter just after two nights of rain; then it was muddy, and anyone could see was not in a natural state, now though almost as rapid and deep its clear waters do not give the angry look it had then — so much for summer and its softening effects.

The road from Stanislaus over broad prairies of poor sandy soil extends for miles until nearing the edge of the line of beautiful old oaks that fringe French Creek and its swamps; then the earth becomes richer and sends up a growth of clover and beautiful grass knee high, until you reach Stockton. Indeed all the best lands of the San Joaquin River are admirably suited for planting with proper drainage and cultivation.

The sea breeze at this season is cold and searching, keeping the thermometer at 60 degrees and 62 degrees for days; when a lull comes the heat is at once oppressive, and the mercury rises to 80 degrees or 85 degrees, and the heat dances before us almost in palpable shapes; the water all stagnant sends its odor of decaying vegetation everywhere, accompanied by myriads of mosquitoes. These conditions exist for miles over the east side, towards the mountains of the San Joaquin.

April 16th.   I am still at Stockton making various excursions with Layton and his friend Howard from New Orleans, and sketching constantly and steadily.   I am indeed crowding all sail to start for home on the steamer which sails on June 1st, with Capt. Patterson.   I have made nearly ninety careful sketches, and many hasty ones, the most interesting I have been able to find in these southern mines, and expect to leave in a few days for Sacramento.

Stockton, April 18th.   I am hardly fit to write for I have just had most melancholy news from Simson.   Lieut. Browning, my dear and devoted friend; to whom I owe a debt of gratitude which I can never pay, for his friendship and kindness to me last year, from the hour that he took my hand on the accursed Rio Grande River until we parted in San Francisco, has been drowned. With Lieuts. Bache and Blunt he was examining the coast near Trinidad Bay, and on attempting to land, the boat "broached to" in the breakers and capsized.   Five were drowned, among them Lieuts. Browning and Bache.   Thus is added another victim to our ill-fated expedition.   Strange that from first to last we have been so fatally followed.   Night after night Browning and I shared the same tent, the same blankets; we knew each [other] well, we were friends.

April 23d. The whole country to the north and east of Stockton through to the Calaveras is most rich and splendid soil, but in many places too low for farming, but the grazing was excellent, quantities of wild oats, rye grass (I think), clover and a species resembling red-top. In many places the grasses were breast high as I waded through them but generally full knee-deep. As we neared the Calaveras we lost our way trying to avoid some bad arroyos, and followed a trail off to the eastward, perhaps three miles, and the country if changed at all, changed for the better. Finding the trend of the trail we were following did not suit our ideas of direction, we turned back at even more than a right angle, and in half an hour entered a wood of open timber, with here and there a lagoon or quagmire of mud and mire; but we worked through and Layton went ahead to reconnoitre, and in about twenty minutes reported the river, which we followed down on a good firm cattle trail, and in half an hour more had come to the upper settlement of the ferry, and were stopped by the fences of newly made farms, and again driven to the swamps to get only a few hundred yards down to the ferry.

We crossed the river after having assisted some Germans with about six hundred sheep, and camped for the night tired enough, having made only about ten miles, but walked nearly twenty of hard travel.

April 24th. As the traveller leaves the north side of the Calaveras and rises higher, the ground becomes cold and has a bluish-looking clay for the road, almost as hard as soft brick, and more tenacious; there are streaks of sandy soil, and in a few places good land; this is scarce however, between the Calaveras and Mokulumne where the Sacramento road crosses the plain. The last three miles of the road is through a pleasant, half-wooded country of live-oak and a few varieties of other shrubs, for the whole of the wood is small.

The sandy road was a great relief to us after the lumpy one of the morning, and we tramped merrily on, until we reached the Mokulumne, and saw a comfortable (for this country), log and jacal built house, and passing about two hundred yards further on, spread our blankets under some half dozen magnificent oaks, and after washing away the dust and heat in the clear, cold little river, very rapid but smooth, ate our lunch of fried pork and bread, and stretched ourselves out to rest for an hour, when we packed up, and being ferried across in a pretty good flat-boat, the only one between Stockton and Sacramento, we continued our walk to Dry Creek over just the same description of country we had had in the morning; but it became more sandy if anything, and towards evening was more of a rolling country. Before we camped for the night we swam "Riley" across a creek about twenty feet wide, and paid one dollar and fifty cents for ourselves and belongings to cross in a sort of canoe, which took us about five minutes.

At the ferry house was a comfortable looking woman with four little children, one an infant; like the Texans she told us they had plenty of cattle, but only one milch cow, so we went on.

April 25th. This morning mounting a slight rise of ground we at once found ourselves on a high dry, too dry, prairie, facing a bracing northwest wind, just strong enough to feel it stirring up our spirits, and we went cheerily on for about eight miles to a bridge, crossed it, and for about two miles had a succession of sloughs to cross, some boggy, some quicksand, others we had to swim. By carefully sounding we kept our packs dry in crossing, and safely reached the back of Murphy's corrall, where I skinned a magpie I had shot, and Layton took a nap. We then went to admire Mr. Murphy's fine stock of brood mares, and the young horses he is raising. At three in the afternoon we packed and left for Sacramento City, keeping to the road for eight miles, when we came to a wood where we collected sufficient fuel for our evening cooking, and went on two miles or so to a lagoon of excellent water, and camped. We had no tent poles, so did as we had done often before, spread one side of the tent on the ground and laid our blankets on that, and covered ourselves with the other part; a corner was put over my gun used as a pole, which gave a place to sit, and also protected our solitary candle from the wind, so we ate our supper in comfort, and enjoyed a kill-deer and a couple of snipe we had shot.

We did not hear a sound but the croakings of hundreds of frogs from the pond by our side. Our long campings out had accustomed us to solitudes like this, but on our desolate, half starving march of last year, doubt, anxiety, yes and fear, had always taken from the complete enjoyment of such freedom as this. The country was so flat that the horizon was lost even in the bright moonlight, and the perfect silence, the pure cloudless sky overhead, the quiet little lake, tended to make everything full of solemnity and peace.

April 26th. This morning half a gale was blowing from the northwest and we were glad to wear our blanket coats until the sun warmed up the earth. We reached "Sutter's Fort" at noon, and lay down under the adobe wall to take our lunch. I was disappointed in the view I had hoped to take; here, on a boundless plain, with two or three hospitals around it, stands a sort of rancho, not so good in many respects as those of New Mexico, but all in the same style, the sides being a series of rooms, one corner being better fitted up for the rancher and his family.

Under some grand old oaks three hundred feet to the eastward, is a cemetery containing a number of graves all made, they tell me, last year when miners and emigrants alike succumbed to illness brought on in many cases by exposure, poor food, and, in some cases, doubtless by disappointed hopes.

Sacramento City is a country village built on a flat point, between a lagoon and the river just below the junction of American River, so low as to be eighteen inches under average high water mark. It has been a source of such speculations as '36 never heard of. I was shown a plot of some half-dozen half lots, which cost last fall two hundred and fifty dollars. The gentleman who owned them, Dr. Pierson, told me he had sold two of them, about a quarter of the whole, for three thousand five hundred dollars, after holding them six months. Truly people did come to California to make money, and some made it, but California will for the present lower the moral tone of all who come here.

There are few refining influences and men become coarse and profane in language, while the hard life does not improve the temper; the sight of the gold they see dug, and the fortunes they hear of that have been made in months, some few even in weeks, make them avaricious.

Many lots of land, valued last year at one thousand dollars, are now valued at ten thousand dollars, but sooner or later the fall must come.

Sutter's Fort appears to have been built with great care as to its means of defence, though at first sight a visitor would be puzzled to know why it was called a fort at all; closer examination shows that it once had, from all appearances, four square towers, some twenty-five feet high, one at each corner, each tower mounting four, eighteen, or at most, twenty-four pound carronades, and the effect of these on the Indians was all that was required for protection, for the Indians here are a very low class and poor race, far inferior to the eastern tribes, and like the Mexicans cowardice is their chief trait, or at least their most prominent one; and if Mr. Sutter could have had twenty faithful followers, he must have been "monarch of all he surveyed."

The swampy neighborhood, bad atmosphere, and malarial conditions must render this section of country unhealthy to a great degree for half the year; for as autumn comes on the daily supply of freshly-melted snow-water from the mountains will no longer purify the lagoons and bayous of the vicinity.

Fever and ague is very prevalent now, and dysentery feared by all. Many of the farmers I find here tell me they are only working to get

"A Dry Gulch" at Coloma, Sutter's Mills
May 2, 1850

money enough to get back with, and that nothing would induce them to settle here. They have unfortunately not seen the lower part of the valley and what lies about Los Angeles and to the south-ward — that is the flower of California.

April 29th. Alas, is it for good or for bad luck, that I have just learned that Layton and myself cannot travel with safety across the country here, as below, on account of the ill-will of the Indians, and that a party of less than six will be unsafe up and across the middle fork of the American River. How stories of Indians are told to every traveller. Though often near them, I have never found any who were not greater cowards than myself, and we leave today for Sutter's Mills, Georgetown, etc., in good health and spirits.

May 4th. Coloma. "Sutter's Mills" is about fifty miles [distant], nearly east of Sacramento. The road to it after passing the first four or five miles runs through a sandy soil, covered at present with what we call "sneeze-weed." There is no water, until after leaving the river, American Fork, we crossed a pretty little "spring branch" as it would be called in Louisiana. The grass is sparse and poor along the whole route, and the face of nature looks like August in the eastern states, so completely that as the refreshing cool breezes come to us each morning, I almost fancy it is the first of September. But in the valleys and on the hillsides the heat is most oppressive, though, as in England, if you stand still for only a few moments in the shade, you soon feel chilled through.

The valley here is not as wide as at Stockton by at least twenty miles, and the grand masses of snow covered mountains seem almost within a day of you, whilst south you still have distance to give additional enchantment to the view. The oaks here are small, not more than from eighteen inches to two feet in diameter; if the soil in which they grew had any richness, I should say the whole forest was of forty years growth at most, but for the occasional presence of a grove of magnificent pines, from a hundred to nearly two hundred feet high. I have measured many at the angle on the ground and have proved it with rods so that I know I am very nearly correct in my statement.

May 6th. Crossing the river at Coloma, on a good bridge, we commenced our ascent of the long and in many places very steep hill. We found a start at dawn would have been much better than at ten, which it now was, as our poor mule "Riley" felt the heat greatly; but with occasional pauses up we went, passing wrecked wagons and broken pack-saddles in several of the narrow parts of the cañons that the road wound through. We were not sorry when we found we had reached the last hill and mounted it, hoping to be repaid by some distant view, but on no side could we see more than a few miles; and we journeyed on, wondering who would be[1] at the mushroom town, Coloma, renowned for being the place where gold was first found by the whites.

We were told that Captain Sutter had made a large fortune by digging gold with many of the Indians he had about him; how true the story is, of course, I cannot say.

[*No date.*] Starting early we had time enough to reach Georgetown, and after the first few miles, were pleased to see a most favorable change in the forest we passed through. A better class of white oaks appeared, and following up a beautiful little creek we gradually came to a pine growth large and magnificent; both yellow and white pine were there, also the long coned pine, and many superb cedars over a hundred feet high. In many places these trees were felled, and split into laths and joists so straight and fine that but little dressing was requisite to fit them for the buildings here constructed, frame houses one storey high. I saw some maples, very like what we call "soft" maple, an elm or two, and many specimens of Nuttall's splendid dogwood in full bloom.

The ultramarine jay is here by dozens, robins, fly catchers, chats, finches by hundreds. I see daily

---

[1] The text is here slightly confused. Perhaps Audubon wondered what would become of the "mushroom town" through which he had just passed.

new birds and plants that a year's steady work could not draw, but if our government would send good men, what a work of national pride could be brought out! Geology, botany, entomology, zoölogy, etc. The views are frequently superb, and the hemlocks and pines of many species most beautiful.

We reached Georgetown — two rows of poor houses and sheds. The houses all one storey, but some with piazzas, and here we took our supper at the "Pine settlement" as it is called.

APPENDIX

[Extract from the New York "Evening Express," February 9, 1849.]

A COMPANY of young men started yesterday afternoon, who, under the command of Major H. L. Webb and J. W. Audubon, will take the land route via Corpus Christi, Monterey, etc., to the gold regions of California. The whole company will number one hundred. Thirty-five or forty went from Philadelphia yesterday.

They proceed direct to Cairo, which is the rendez-vous of the party; here they will be joined by companies from the West. At New Orleans or thereabouts as most convenient, they will purchase

---

[1] The number of persons in the company varied widely at different times. About eighty started from New York. The list, here reprinted from the New York "Evening Express," contains seventy-five names but does not claim to be complete. Apparently a number of men from Philadelphia, but not as many as stated above, joined the company, since it is repeatedly described as "at one time numbering ninety-eight." The implication in the *Journal* that there were but sixty-five at Cairo must be an error. About fifty started from Roma with Mr. Audubon but the number reached fifty-seven at Parras. One subsequently died, another remained at Mapimi three left the company at Ures, eleven took the boat from San Diego and "about forty" continued the march to Los Angeles. This seems to have been the number of the reunited company in San Francisco, of whom thirty-eight, including Mr. Audubon, made the tour of the southern mines.

mules, horses and all necessary equipments, each man finding his own outfit.

We append a list of the names of those who go from here in this company, so far as known.

Audubon, John W.
Ayres, Venancia
Bachman, Jacob H.
Barclay, William B.
Benson, Leffert L.
Benson, Robert, Jr.
Black, John A.
Bloomfield, John J.
Boden, Hamilton J.
Brady, Henry
Brady, John
Cararley, John
Clement, James B.
Combs, Frederick S.
Cowden, Henry
Cree, William J.
Damon, Luke
Davis, Geradus T.
Delancy, John
Doubleday, Ulysses
Elmslie, James D.
Ely, Justin, Jr.
Graham, Charles Montrose

Graham, A. Clason
Graham, A. Spencer
Hall, Thomas H., Jr.
Havens, Langdon H.
Hinckley, Lyman T.
Hudson, David
Hutchinson, William A.
Kashon, Israel
Kearney, John, M. D.
Lambert, Edward A.
Lambert, John B.
Lambert, John S.
Lambert, Joseph
Lambert, J. Robert
Lee, Augustus T.
Liscomb, Samuel H.
Liscomb, William H.
Mallory, Henry C.
McCusker, Peter
McGown, Andrew J.
Molinear, William D.
Nevin, Andrew M.
Osgood, E. W.
Plumb, John H.

Powell, Emmett

Rodgers, J. Kearney, Jr.

Sherwood, James W.

Sherwood, Richard W.

Shipman, Aaron T.

Sloat, Lewis M.

Steele, George D.

Stevens, John

Stille, Henry

Stivers, Daniel A.

Stivers, William D.

Tallman, Harmon

Tone, John H.

Trask, John B., M. D.

Valentine, Charles

Valentine, Thomas B.

Valentine, Matthias B.

Van Buren, George T.

Watkinson, Joseph S.

Walsh, Nicholas J.

Warner, James

Webb, Edward C.

Webb, Watson

Weed, George

Whittlesey, Gilbert B.

Whittlesey, William

Williamson, Isaac H.

Winthrop, Francis B.

INDEX

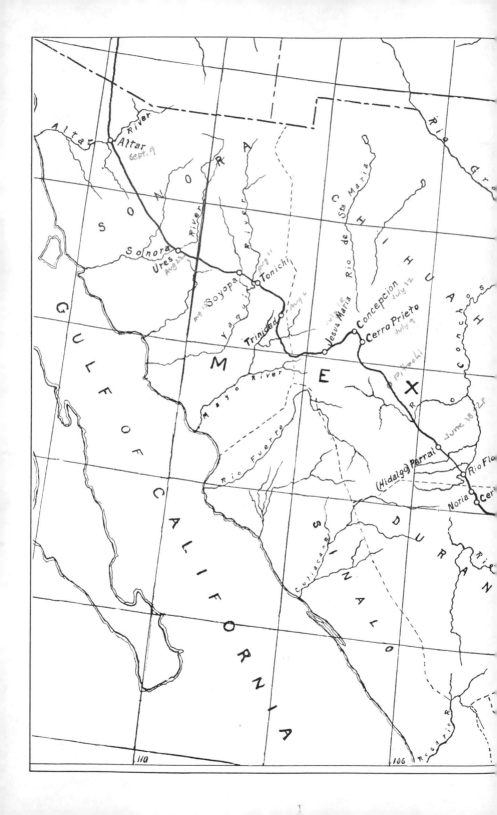

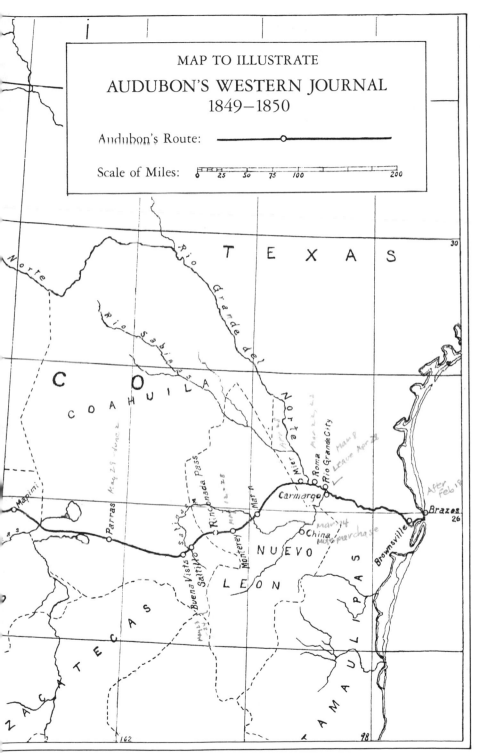

MAP TO ILLUSTRATE

AUDUBON'S WESTERN JOURNAL
1849–1850

Audubon's Route:

Scale of Miles: 0 25 50 75 100 200

(Map continued on following pages)

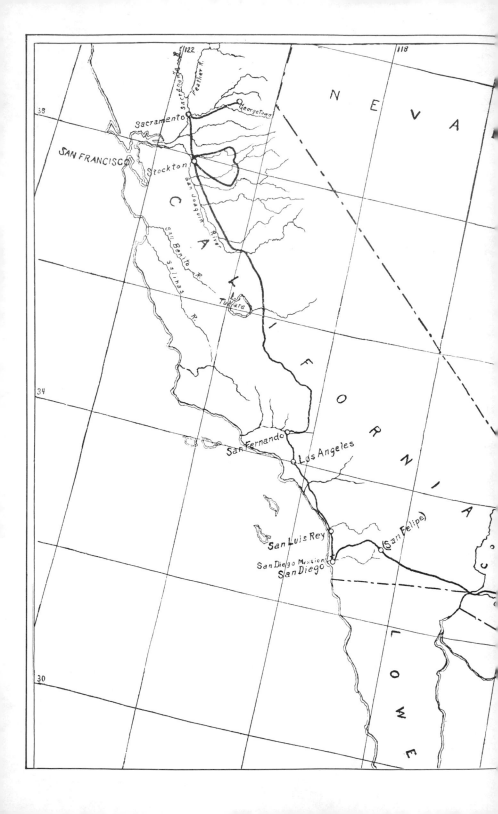

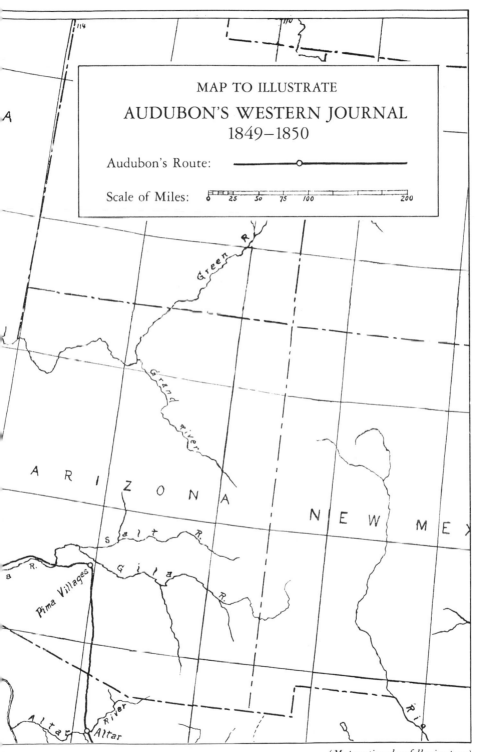

MAP TO ILLUSTRATE

AUDUBON'S WESTERN JOURNAL
1849–1850

Audubon's Route:

Scale of Miles:

(*Map continued on following page*)

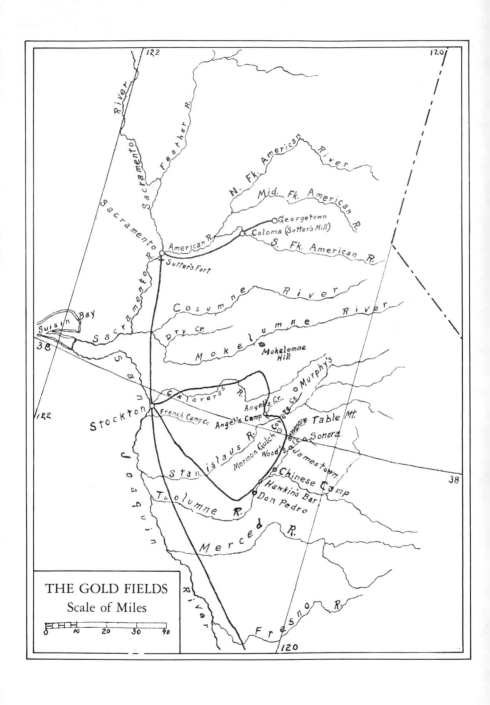

THE GOLD FIELDS
Scale of Miles